Galatians

Discover Together Bible Study Series

Psalms: Discovering Authentic Worship
Proverbs: Discovering Ancient Wisdom for a Postmodern World, Volume 1
Proverbs: Discovering Ancient Wisdom for a Postmodern World, Volume 2
Ecclesiastes: Discovering Meaning in a Meaningless World
Daniel: Discovering the Courage to Stand for Your Faith
Hosea: Discovering God's Fierce Love
Luke: Discovering Healing in Jesus' Words to Women
Galatians: Discovering Freedom in Christ Through Daily Practice
Ephesians: Discovering Your Identity and Purpose in Christ
Philippians: Discovering Joy Through Relationship
James: Discovering God's Delight in a Lived-Out Faith
1 Peter: Discovering Encouragement in Troubling Times
Revelation: Discovering Life for Today and Eternity

Leader's guides are available at www.discovertogetherseries.com

A Discover Together BIBLE STUDY

Galatians

Discovering Freedom in Christ Through Daily Practice

Sue Edwards &
Jodie Niznik

Kregel
Publications

Galatians: Discovering Freedom in Christ Through Daily Practice

Published by Kregel Publications, a division of Kregel Inc., 2450 Oak Industrial Dr. NE, Grand Rapids, MI 49505.

ISBN 978-0-8254-4441-8

Printed in the United States of America

19 20 21 22 23 24 25 26 27 / 8 7 6 5 4 3 2

Contents

How to Get the Most Out of a Discover Together Bible Study

Women today need Bible study to keep balanced, focused, and Christ-centered in their busy worlds. The tiered questions in *Galatians: Discovering Freedom in Christ Through Daily Practice* allow you to choose a depth of study that fits your lifestyle, which may even vary from week to week, depending on your schedule.

Just completing the basic questions will require about one and a half hours per lesson, and will provide a basic overview of the text. For busy women, this level offers in-depth Bible study with a minimum time commitment.

"Digging Deeper" questions are for those who want to, and make time to, probe the text even more deeply. Answering these questions may require outside resources such as an atlas, Bible dictionary, or concordance; you may be asked to look up parallel passages for additional insight; or you may be encouraged to investigate the passage using an interlinear Greek-English text or *Vine's Expository Dictionary.* This deeper study will challenge you to learn more about the history, culture, and geography related to the Bible, and to grapple with complex theological issues and differing views. Some with teaching gifts and an interest in advanced academics will enjoy exploring the depths of a passage, and might even find themselves creating outlines and charts and writing essays worthy of seminarians!

This inductive Bible study is designed for both individual and group discovery. You will benefit most if you tackle each week's lesson on your own, and then meet with other women to share insights, struggles, and aha moments. Bible study leaders will find a free, downloadable leader's guide for each study, along with general tips for leading small groups, at www.discovertogetherseries.com.

Choose a realistic level of Bible study that fits your schedule. You may want to finish the basic questions first, and then "dig deeper" as time permits. Take time to savor the questions, and don't rush through the application. Read the sidebars for additional insight to enrich the experience. Note the optional passage to memorize and determine if this discipline would be helpful for you. Do not allow yourself to be intimidated by women who have more time or who are gifted differently.

Make your Bible study—whatever level you choose—top priority. Consider spacing your study throughout the week so that you can take time to ponder and meditate on what the Holy Spirit is teaching you. Do not make other appointments during the group Bible study. Ask God to enable you to attend faithfully. Come with an excitement to learn from others and a desire to share yourself and your journey. Give it your best, and God promises to join you on this adventure that can change your life.

PRACTICE SECTIONS

If you've done a Discover Together Bible study before, you'll notice a new feature in Galatians. Each week the lesson will include a short practice section—activities many call "spiritual disciplines" or "soul training." We like the word *practice*, though, because it's simple and expresses the idea that you are trying something out in your relationship with the Lord. You are just practicing. This section provides an opportunity to reflect on the lessons you are learning and apply them in a new way. These practices won't take huge amounts of time, but they require some planning. Therefore, each lesson opens with the practice section. Read it through and create a personal plan to try the suggested activities for the week.

You'll discover practices you love in these sections—things that bring new life into your relationship with God. Some of these exercises may be hard and others easy, even fun, but each will help you stretch and grow, which makes the effort totally worth it.

I learned that the spiritual disciplines are God's means of training us, finite and flawed creatures, to love the invisible, almighty, infinite Creator; they are the means by which we learn to enjoy him; they are the means God uses to nurture our confidence in his goodness and love.

Through the spiritual disciplines God not only touched me, he gripped me hard in a fist that is stronger than a lion's paw. He pulled me close against his heart and taught me to discern the rhythms of grace.

—Jan Winebrenner (*Intimate Faith*, 5)

Why Study Galatians?

The best way to truly grasp God's grace, his special favor, is to bathe yourself in Paul's letter to the Galatians. The whole letter is one argument after another for amazing grace. If you haven't embraced this freedom yet, we pray you'll discover truths that will revolutionize your life for God's magnificent glory and your overwhelming joy. If you've been a Christian for many years, dig deep into this marvelous book, and you'll discover nuances of grace that you've never seen before.

JODIE'S STORY

I became a Christian the summer I turned thirteen. I had never attended church, so I had no context for my new faith. I misconstrued God to be a big, bossy judge in the sky who was just waiting for me to trip up. And trip up I did, over and over. I imagined God crossing his arms, sighing loudly, and swiveling his back to me, so I would start to negotiate. I would beg him to take me back and I'd make all kinds of unattainable promises to do better next time. Of course, my "doing better" never lasted.

My sad misunderstanding of God led to a horribly unhealthy relationship. So I gave up. I walked away at age fifteen and then again at nineteen. But that didn't work either. I could not ignore the deep longing and emptiness in my soul.

Finally, at twenty, I met some people who had healthy relationships with the Lord. They weren't shouldering the same burdens I was. Their faith wasn't contingent upon their actions; rather, their actions flowed from their faith. And they exuded joy—the complete opposite of what I experienced in my relationship with the Lord.

The more time I spent with them, the more I learned some essential truths about God's unconditional love for me. But there was still a nagging sense of guilt that I was always letting him down. I believed he loved me because he had to, not because he wanted to.

I didn't know how to live out my relationship with God. I knew I was supposed to live differently, but since I didn't know how, I just mimicked what I saw others doing. The actions weren't necessarily wrong, but the motivation was. I was still jumping through hoops hoping to please God.

A few years later I took an intensive class at my church, and that's when I started to understand the truth of living by the grace of God instead of the law of God. These truths seeped into my heart and ultimately transformed our relationship. I was finally set free from my burden of trying to do things to please God. And then something beautiful started to happen: instead of serving God and others out of fear or obligation, I started serving out of love, empowered by the Holy Spirit.

To the outside observer, my life looked exactly the same, as I did many of the same things. But my motivation had completely changed, and so my interior life was dramatically different. I was transformed. My actions flowed out of love.

SUE'S STORY

I was an unplanned, unwanted only child. My grandparents on both sides of my family were Christians but their churches were mired in legalism. As a result, my parents evaded everything Christian and I grew up feeling unloved and vulnerable.

When I was twenty-four, after several years of searching for God in all the wrong places, Jesus found me when a neighbor invited me to a women's Bible study. As the women there re-mothered me, I fell in love with Jesus. They taught me my value in Christ. He healed my marriage and revealed my purpose—to serve through teaching the Bible and ministering to women.

But when I subsequently discovered the real meaning of grace and the freedom it brings, my Christian life exploded in passion and joy for Jesus. Before then I had tried to obey the rules and, like Jodie, the harder I tried, the more I messed up. I didn't understand that Jesus loved me even then. My misunderstanding eventually led to depression. The real cure came when I truly grasped grace, gave myself permission to be in process, and began living out of gratitude for what Christ had done for me. I surrendered to the Holy Spirit, giving him permission to lead and empower me.

The American Banking Association once sponsored a two-week training program to help tellers detect counterfeit bills. The program was unique—never during the two-week training did the tellers even look at a counterfeit bill, nor did they listen to any lectures concerning the characteristics of counterfeit bills. . . . All they did for two weeks was handle authentic currency, hour after hour and day after day, until they were so familiar with the true that they could not possibly be fooled by the false.

That is also the biblical approach to dealing with spiritual counterfeits. The idea is to become so familiar with the real thing, by meditating on it, praying about it and acting it out in everyday life, that the counterfeit can be recognized immediately.

—Ben Patterson, *Waiting*, 153

INTRODUCTION

We're convinced that we don't study Galatians nearly enough. Because when we are set free to live in the power of the Holy Spirit and live out Christ's law of love, we are unstoppable.

Before we study any book of Scripture, it's important to spend a few minutes exploring the author, date, location, and original audience of the book. An understanding of the original intent of the letter can significantly help us understand its meaning for us today. With this in mind, we encourage you to take a few minutes to watch the intro video before you continue.

Introduction to Studying Galatians *(10:52 minutes)*.

Stay strong in your study of Galatians over the next nine lessons—you are in for incredible blessings!

Understanding the Law | LESSON 1

PRACTICE ❀ REST

When we aren't getting proper rest, we don't function well. We become more forgetful and irritable. We know we need rest, yet we often try to cheat sleep by staying up a little later or getting up a little earlier.

The National Sleep Foundation tells us that adults need seven to nine hours of sleep every night (Hirshkowitz et al.). A quick search on WebMD will tell you that lack of sleep contributes to a myriad of problems, such as depression, heart issues, forgetfulness, weight gain, and accidents. We need sufficient rest. We can only fight against our God-given design so long before we reap serious consequences.

This week we are going to start our study with one of our favorite spiritual practices: rest. This practice reflects the gospel message Paul teaches in Galatians.

Since we are saved by grace through faith in Christ, we can and should rest.

At least one night this week, go to bed at a reasonable time and sleep until your body wakes up.

This may take some planning—especially if you have young children or other responsibilities that necessitate you getting up during the night or early in the morning. If that's the case, ask your spouse or a trusted friend for help.

If a long night of sleep is simply impossible for your schedule and life, choose two or more nights when you will intentionally go to bed earlier to try to maximize your sleep.

Many of us struggle to sleep through the night. If you do wake up, take a few deep breaths and pray for the Lord to help you return to sleep. If you continue waking up, see your physician for help.

This practice isn't meant to put pressure on you to accomplish anything; it's about you getting rest that will refresh and renew.

OPTIONAL

Memorize
Romans 3:23–24

All have sinned and fall short of the glory of God, and all are justified freely by his grace through the redemption that came by Christ Jesus.

After completing the exercise, reflect on your experience by answering these questions:

- How did you like this sleep activity? What was challenging?

- What did you notice about the day after your practice of rest (your reactions, productivity, alertness, energy level, etc.)?

- What parallels do you see between faith and the act of sleeping?

To recap what was covered in the introduction video (see page 11), here is a snapshot of the letter to the Galatians:

Author: Paul
Date and Recipients: Written around AD 48 to the churches in southern Galatia
Purpose: To discredit the heretical teaching that followers of Jesus also need to follow the Mosaic law

To understand Paul's arguments in Galatians, we must first understand the Old Testament covenants and the Mosaic law. We're going to spend this lesson examining some Old Testament passages to give us a basic understanding of these covenants, the Mosaic law, and why some were struggling to let go of keeping the law.

Read Galatians 1:1–9.

THE OLD COVENANT AND THE LAW

As soon as Adam and Eve fell for Satan's temptation and sinned, God started revealing his plan for restoration and redemption. We catch our first glimpse of this plan in Genesis 3:15. As God curses the serpent (Satan) he says that someone will come who will "crush [the serpent's] head." That someone is Jesus. And to be clear, no one survives a head-crushing. God is telling Satan his days are numbered. Jesus will defeat sin and death. The next time God specifically talks about his redemptive plan is to Abraham in Genesis 12.

1. Read Genesis 12:2–3. This is known as the Abrahamic covenant, a covenant God made with Abraham (called Abram in this passage). How many times does God say "I will" in this passage?

Notice that the Abrahamic covenant is a **unilateral** and **unconditional** covenant because it depends on God and not on what Abraham does or does not do.

DIGGING DEEPER

Using a dictionary, define *unilateral* and *bilateral* as it would relate to a treaty or promise.

2. Who does God say will be blessed through Abraham? Do you think this applies to you too? Why or why not?

Genesis 12:2–3 are significant verses. God is setting the stage for salvation to include all people, not just the nation of Israel.

Now let's turn to the law.

3. Read Exodus 19:3–6, noticing the words *if* and *then*. Verses 5–6 are known as the Mosaic covenant. God gave this covenant to Moses specifically for the nation of Israel. What is God offering to the nation of Israel if they obey?

Notice that the Mosaic covenant is a **bilateral** and **conditional** covenant because it depends on the actions of two parties. If one party doesn't uphold their end of the deal, the other party is released from their obligation.

4. Read Exodus 24:4–8. How did the nation of Israel respond to God's offer?

5. Scan Deuteronomy 28, paying special attention to verses 1–2 and 15. What kind of blessings did God say he would give the nation if they obeyed? What kind of curses would he give the nation if they disobeyed? Are these blessings and curses material and physical, or will they be given after death?

6. Complete this chart to summarize what you have learned so far about the Abrahamic covenant and the Mosaic covenant.

Covenant	Type of covenant	Who did the covenant include?	What did it depend upon?	What was promised?
Abrahamic		All people		All people will be blessed through Abraham
Mosaic	Bilateral		Obedience to "the law"	Earthly blessings or curses for Israel

Not all "if . . . then" systems are bad. Sometimes they are quite valid and helpful. For example, if I don't show up to work, then I will lose my job. That's a valid "if . . . then" principle. "If . . . then" systems become destructive, however, when they are imposed on relationships. For example, if a child receives conditional "if . . . then" love from a parent, he or she will end up insecure, unstable, and in need of significant counseling. We thrive and grow when we know we are unconditionally loved. This is what parents should offer us and this is what God absolutely offers us.

7. What are some areas of your life in which you operate on an "if . . . then" system (for example, if you go to work, then you get paid; if you eat your dinner, then you get dessert)? Which of these "if . . . then" systems are valid and helpful? Which are destructive? Why?

8. Describe an "if . . . then" relationship you've experienced personally or witnessed. (No names, please.) How did this relationship suffer?

9. In what ways can an "if . . . then" system be wrongly imposed on your relationship with God? What happens when this occurs?

Paul uses the term *law* to refer specifically to the Mosaic covenant. The law includes not only the Ten Commandments (Exodus 20) but also additional laws that regulated diet, holiness, and worship. All together 613 laws regulated Jewish life. We will look specifically at the Ten Commandments, but realize that Paul refers to much more when he uses the term *law.*

THE PURPOSE OF THE LAW

The law created a system that the Israelites were supposed to follow to relate to God and one another. However, the law was never intended to be a means to earn salvation. It was always a means of blessings or curses within salvation.

10. To discover some of the purposes of the law, match the following verses with their purpose.

__ Deuteronomy 4:6–7	A. To instruct the next generation
__ Deuteronomy 6:6–7	B. To guard and protect us until Jesus came
__ Romans 7:7	C. To reveal or expose our sin
__ Galatians 3:24	D. To evangelize, showing other nations the greatness of God.

11. In Romans 7:7, Paul says the law exposed his sin. Can you think of any current laws in our society that tend to expose you as a lawbreaker?

12. Read Ecclesiastes 7:20 and Romans 3:10–12. What do these verses say about mankind? Based on your answer, do you think anyone would be able to perfectly keep the law?

THE DURATION OF THE LAW

13. According to Galatians 3:19 and 24–25, how long was the law supposed to last?

THE NEW COVENANT

14. Read Hebrews 8:7–12, where a new covenant is promised. According to Hebrews 8:7–9, what was wrong with the Mosaic covenant and why?

15. How many times does God say "I will" in Hebrews 8:10 and 12?

What kind of covenant is this (unilateral or bilateral) and, therefore, who is this covenant dependent upon?

DIGGING DEEPER

The new covenant in Hebrews 8:7–12 was originally stated in Jeremiah. Read Jeremiah 31:31–34. What do you learn about God and his future plans for Israel and the world?

What will God do with our sins?

16. According to Hebrews 9:15 and Luke 22:20, who brings about the new covenant? How?

The old covenant law was written externally, on tablets of stone (Exodus 31:18), yet the new covenant is written internally, on our hearts (Hebrews 8:10).

17. To help us understand the difference between old-covenant living and new-covenant living, think about a recent time someone told you what to do. How did you react? Now think about a recent time you decided on your own to do a similar action. How did it feel to do the same action on your own initiative? What was different? Did the actual action look any different?

DIGGING DEEPER

Read Luke 2:22–35. What happened in the passage? Analyze Simeon's blessing to discover more about the extent of new-covenant blessing. What do you learn?

18. Rewrite Ephesians 3:6 in your own words. Hebrews 8:10 seems to indicate that the new covenant is made with the people of Israel, yet we see here that Jesus came for all people—Jews and non-Jews (who are called Gentiles in Scripture). How does Ephesians 3:6 explain this new information? Why do you think God kept the salvation of the Gentiles a "mystery"?

19. Fill in the chart below, adding what you've learned about the new covenant. (Note: this is the same chart we started in question 6.)

Covenant	Type of covenant	Who did the covenant include?	What did it depend upon?	What was promised?	Additional thoughts and notes
Abrahamic	Unilateral	All people	God	All people will be blessed through Abraham	
Mosaic	Bilateral	Israel	Obedience to "the law"	Earthly blessings or curses for Israel	Jesus fulfilled the law
New covenant				God will put his law in our hearts; we will be his people; he will forgive and forget our sins	Jesus brought the new covenant

RESISTING THE NEW WAY

20. Try to place yourself in the shoes of an Old Testament Israelite. What do you think it would have been like living under the law of the old covenant? Were there any perks? (Look back at question 5 to help you answer this.)

21. The law set the Jewish people apart from all the other nations. It gave them boundaries and guidelines. It prescribed a way of life. Considering this, why do you think it was hard for them to let go of the law?

22. Review what you've studied in this lesson. Write down some of the things you learned or were reminded of. Write down any questions that surfaced. (We will learn more about the law throughout the study, especially in lesson 6. Capture your questions here so you don't forget them.)

Once a pastor told me that works and grace were two sides of the same coin, and you couldn't have one without the other. Another pastor once explained in a sermon that God gives us the rowboat but we have to row it—that's how we are redeemed. Both were sincere, but according to Scripture both were dead wrong. I'm so grateful that God's Word is clear: we are saved by grace through faith alone in Christ alone. None of us can take any credit for our salvation. Now I live every day out of gratitude for the indescribable gift of my sweet relationship with God, my heavenly Father, through Jesus Christ, the glorious Son, and by the powerful Holy Spirit who strengthens me to live for him every moment. Praise God for his magnificent grace! —Sue

The Christian is not under law which should be a relief to all of us. We can all take great comfort in the fact that we are no longer bound to keep dietary laws, circumcision, or strict Sabbath regulations. However, many want to still claim the promise of material blessings found in these laws. We simply can't have it both ways. When the requirements of law went away as the standard of relationship with God, so did the promise of material blessing for keeping this law. That doesn't mean God doesn't still bless some people with material wealth; it just means he isn't doing it because of their obedience to the law. —Jodie

Grace, Peace, and Astonishment

LESSON 2

PRACTICE ✿ MEDIA FAST

Paul starts out Galatians with a prayer for the recipient to experience grace and peace from God.

Grace, peace—beautiful words bursting with meaning. Let's focus on peace.

Peace is the absence of strife and a state of calm. Unfortunately, we often experience too much strife and never enjoy enough calm. Something always threatens to steal our peace.

This week we are going to do a media fast.

Media can refer to the device itself—the means through which something is conveyed, like a smartphone—or to mass media—communication for the masses, such as news feeds. Either can disturb our peace! We are going to try to reclaim a little peace this week by untethering from our smartphones and laptops. We encourage you to lay aside your mobile device for one week to strive to be present and embrace a few quiet moments.

We know our devices are essential to how many of us live. There are legitimate reasons for us to remain semi-attached. But there is a difference between picking up your device from nervous habit rather than because the phone is ringing. So, instead of checking, checking, checking, take a deep breath and put the device down.

If you don't have a mobile device you're attached to, consider how you occupy yourself or fritter away your free moments. Is there something you could lay aside instead?

Take a moment right now to make a plan. Decide how you will and will not use your devices. We hope you will take up this challenge.

We're praying, "grace and peace to you from God our Father and the Lord Jesus Christ" (Galatians 1:3)!

OPTIONAL

Memorize Romans 8:1–2

Therefore, there is now no condemnation for those who are in Christ Jesus, because through Christ Jesus the law of the Spirit who gives life has set you free from the law of sin and death.

After completing the exercise, reflect on your experience by answering these questions:

- If you participated in the media fast, how did you choose to do it? Please be specific.

- In what ways did this activity have an impact on your peace?

- What did you learn about God or yourself through this activity?

In the first lesson, we learned about the old covenant and the law. We discovered that there were lots of reasons for the law, but salvation was never one of them. Salvation was and always has been through faith in Jesus. However, a group of false teachers, often called Judaizers, had infiltrated the churches in Galatia to discredit Paul and teach a different way of salvation—the mingling of law with grace. They were saying faith in Jesus wasn't enough—that salvation required Jesus plus works.

Paul is adamant though: faith is through Christ alone. He starts his letter with the mission to reestablish his credibility so he can reestablish the credibility of his message. This is where the book of Galatians begins.

Read Galatians 1:1–5.

PAUL'S AUTHORITY AND THE GOSPEL

1. Paul calls himself "an apostle," which means "one who is sent." Who does Paul specifically say did not send him? Who does Paul say did send him?

In his reference to himself, Paul emphasized his apostolic office. The Greek word translated "apostle" (*apostolos*) means "one who is sent." The New Testament uses this word in two ways: In its more restricted sense, the word means someone who had received a special commission from the risen Christ (i.e., Paul and the twelve apostles). In its more general sense, it refers to those sent with a message from God.
—Thomas Constable (*Notes*, 8)

2. Why is Paul defending his credibility to the Galatians so emphatically?

We can call people who have unusual leadership gifts . . . "small-a" apostles. But Paul is a "capital-A" Apostle, commissioned directly by Jesus. The "capital-A" Apostles had, and have, absolute authority. What *they* write is Scripture.
—Timothy Keller (*Galatians*, 15)

3. How do you determine if a preacher or teacher is credible?

Grace: The undeserved favor of God in providing salvation for those deserving condemnation.
—Jimmy Millikin (*Holman Illustrated Bible Dictionary*)

4. Verses 3–5 are actually a short prayer that Paul prays for the Galatians, which doubles as a greeting. Look up the definitions of grace and peace (a biblical definition of grace is in the margin) and write them in your own words. From whom does Paul say grace and peace come? Why do you think Paul specifically prays these things for the Galatians?

5. Is there an area of your life that lacks peace right now? If so, what is it and why do you think you are struggling to feel peace in this area? Consider sharing this with friends as a prayer request.

6. Reflect on Paul's full prayer in Galatians 1:3–5. How do you know that Jesus forgives your sins? Do you struggle with any sins that you aren't sure Jesus will forgive? If so, what are they? What makes you think Jesus forgives this sin for others but not for you? Pray and ask God to help you accept his forgiveness in these areas.

The Jewish term for peace, *shalom*, means to experience comprehensive wholeness, harmony, and rest in one's relationship with God and the world. The theme of peace is threaded through the whole of Scripture. Peace was disrupted in the garden of Eden and will one day be fully restored when Jesus returns. Until that day, we live in tension. We have peace in our relationship with God through Jesus, yet we still live in a world of strife and sin. Paul, in praying for peace, is drawing from his Jewish heritage and praying for the Galatians to experience wholeness, harmony, and rest in their relationship with God and the world.

Substitution is why the gospel is so revolutionary. Christ's death was not just a general sacrifice, but a substitutionary one. He did not merely buy us a "second chance," giving us another opportunity to get life right and stay right with God. He did *all* we needed to do, but cannot do. If Jesus' death really paid for our sins on our behalf, we can never fall back into condemnation. Why? Because God would then be getting two payments for the same sin, which is unjust!

—Timothy Keller (*Galatians*, 16)

7. Consider the statement that we are "rescued from the present evil age." In what ways have you experienced this truth in your life? In what ways does evil still impact you?

As often happens today, when someone wants to discredit an idea they start with discrediting the messenger. This is obviously what the Judaizers have done. They've poked at Paul's credentials as a way to undermine his message. Thus Paul spends about a third of the letter defending his credibility. He does this not because he's offended by some personal attack, but because he's offended by an attack on the gospel. He knows his credibility is tied to his message.

8. Someday all evil will be banished and we will dwell with God. Read Revelation 21:3–4. How do these verses describe that day? How does this give you hope for the future?

Paul prayed this powerful little prayer for the Galatian church, but it is a prayer for us as well. Because Jesus died for our sins (v. 4) and was resurrected from the dead (v. 1) we are rescued (v. 4). As a result, grace and peace (*shalom*) are extended to us too.

Read Galatians 1:6–10.

WHAT WERE YOU THINKING?

These verses begin the body of the letter and introduce the main issue the book addresses.

9. What have the churches in Galatia done that shocked Paul (v. 6)?

10. The Greek word *thaumazo* is translated "I am astonished," "I am amazed" (NASB), and "I am shocked" (NLT). It was a conventional expression in the Greek that signaled astonishment, rebuke, disapproval, and disappointment (Longenecker, *Galatians*, 11). Think back to a recent time when a loved one veered off course and you experienced *thaumazo*. How did you feel? What did you do? If you handled it poorly, what do you wish you had done differently? If you handled it well, why? Pray and ask God to help you handle *thaumazo* well the next time you experience it.

The gospel message, by its very nature, cannot be changed even slightly without being lost. It's like a vacuum. You can't allow in some air and say that it is now a "90 percent vacuum" or an "air enriched vacuum." It is either a complete vacuum or no vacuum at all! Equally, the message of the gospel is that you are saved by grace through Christ's work and nothing else at all. As soon as you add anything to it, you have lost it entirely. The moment you revise it, you reverse it.

—Timothy Keller (*Galatians*, 22–23)

11. What does verse 7 say the other preachers were doing?

12. *Gospel* simply means "good news." Paul started this letter with the essentials of this good news of our faith in verses 1–5. Review these verses and read 1 Corinthians 15:3–5 (also written by Paul), then list the essentials of the gospel found in these passages.

Galatianism. The attempt to mingle law and grace. Galatianism takes many forms, but sooner or later it always ends up in a meaningless contradiction: "God's grace has made it possible for man to *work for* His acceptance and forgiveness" or "God loves us unconditionally *if* we keep all the rules." Law is the realm of what you *earn* by your performance. Grace is the realm of receiving a *free gift*. How could you ever mingle the two?

—Bob George (*Classic Christianity*, 124)

13. Have you ever experienced someone distorting the essentials of this gospel message? If so, how? If you haven't experienced it firsthand, what are some ways you think someone could distort the gospel essentials?

14. Paul has some pretty weighty words for how teachers of a contrary gospel should be treated. What does he say should happen to them (vv. 8–9)? Why do you think the consequences are so severe? Do you agree with these consequences? Why or why not?

The Judaizers had come along and substituted their false gospel for the true gospel, and for this sin, Paul pronounced them accursed. The word he uses is *anathema*, which means "dedicated to destruction." . . . No matter who the preacher may be—an angel from heaven or even Paul himself—if he preaches any other gospel, he is accursed!
—Warren Wiersbe (*Bible Exposition Commentary*, 684-85)

15. Do you think Paul's consequences apply to our honest misunderstandings of Scripture? Why or why not?

DIGGING DEEPER

Paul wrote about other preachers of the gospel in his letter to the Philippians. Read Philippians 1:12–18 and 3:1–4, 18–21. How does Paul describe the different types of preachers? Which ones does he rejoice over and which ones does he condemn? What are the lessons for us today?

The Disease to Please is a set of self-defeating thoughts and flawed beliefs about yourself and other people that fuel compulsive behavior that, in turn, is driven by the need to avoid forbidden negative feelings. This triple combination of distorted thinking, compulsive behavior, and the need to avoid fearful feelings creates the syndrome of people-pleasing and forms the Disease to Please triangle.
—Harriet Braiker
(*Disease to Please*, 11)

WHO ARE YOU TRYING TO PLEASE?

16. Read Galatians 1:10. Paul finishes this verse saying, "If I were still trying to please people, I would not be a servant of Christ." In what ways might you be letting people-pleasing interfere with serving Christ?

DIGGING DEEPER

Paul also wrote about the amazing grace of God in his letter to the Romans. What do you learn about grace in Romans 5:1–11?

17. Who are some of the people in your life that need to hear the gospel message (friends, family, neighbors, co-workers, etc.)? List a few of their names below. Take a moment to pray for each person you listed and ask Jesus to give you courage to speak the gospel truth boldly and with love the next time the opportunity arises.

Paul has passionately introduced us to the problem of Galatianism—the mingling of the free grace of Christ with works. And he said adamantly that it's not only wrong, it's dangerous. We must remember that we are saved by faith alone in Christ alone.

Credible Messenger, Credible Message

LESSON 3

OPTIONAL

Memorize Galatians 3:26–28

So in Christ Jesus you are all children of God through faith, for all of you who were baptized into Christ have clothed yourselves with Christ. There is neither Jew nor Gentile, neither slave nor free, nor is there male and female, for you are all one in Christ Jesus.

PRACTICE ✿ GENEROSITY

This week we will look deeper into Paul's conversion and calling, and examine two trips he made to Jerusalem—one to establish his independence from the apostles and the second to establish his unity with them.

During this second trip, Paul's main concern was the problem of the Judaizers. Then at the very end of the passage describing this trip, Paul notes something we find interesting. He says, "All they asked was that we should continue to remember the poor" (Galatians 2:10). Paul's primary purpose was to discuss whether Gentiles needed to become Jews before they could become Christ-followers, as signified by circumcision. After they decided this important theological issue, they turned their focus to the poor. This seemingly casual mention amidst the weighty theological discussion should alert us to its significance.

People in need were obviously close to Jesus's heart. A quick search will bring up many examples of Jesus ministering to, healing, and feeding the needy, and now we see the early church continuing to make people in need a priority.

This week let's intentionally look for and respond to people in need, particularly those we cross paths with in our daily lives.

To practice generosity you will need to plan ahead. Start with prayer. Ask God if you should give money, time, or even a possession. Next, prepare. For example, if you decide to give money, you may want to withdraw the amount in cash and keep it with you—ready to respond when you feel prompted.

Ask the Holy Spirit to help you see. Then when you feel a nudge, respond. It could be a woman at the grocery store, a family at the park, a student at Starbucks, or even a longtime friend you have a hunch needs a little help . . . it'll be different for each of us.

A few words of caution: First, don't go into analytical mode—we can't judge the real circumstances of someone by how they appear. Second, you may feel a little vulnerable, foolish, or awkward. You aren't alone. If you are going through this study in a group, it's likely others in your group feel the same. Third, be wise and safe. In other words, please don't pick up the strange man from the side of the road. We really don't want to see your name in the headlines. Finally, be bold. When you feel prompted, take the leap and leave the rest to Jesus.

After completing the exercise, reflect on your experience by answering these questions:

- What did you feel led to do this week?

- What happened as a result? Include thoughts, feelings, reactions.

- What did you learn about yourself or God as you participated in this exercise?

I (Jodie) have never had anyone blatantly attack my credibility.

Well, not really.

I mean, there is this one person. She is always questioning, always telling me I'm not really qualified or good enough, always trying to hold me back. I simply call her the "mean girl." I'm betting you have a mean person in your life too. Most of us do. As you can probably guess, my mean girl is me. She's that voice inside my head that is always whispering lies.

As I grow, I'm learning not to listen to her as much. I'm learning how to fight her lies with truth. And I'm learning how to spot her attacks and silence them a little faster. That doesn't mean she doesn't achieve some victories. But I'm learning.

Paul's credibility is also being attacked, but not from within. The Judaizers are attacking Paul's credibility. They reason, if they can discredit Paul, then they can discredit his message and in turn advance their own. Paul won't stand for it. He's on to their schemes. Unfortunately, it appears that some of the Galatians may be falling for their lies. They are confused. Whom should they believe? In this next section of Scripture Paul defends his credibility; let's discover how.

Read Galatians 1:11–24.

CREDIBILITY AND CONVERSION

1. How does Paul say he received the gospel he preached (v. 12)?

2. The revelation Paul experienced happened through a dramatic encounter with Jesus. Read the account in Acts 9:1–9. (Note: Paul is called Saul in this passage. He receives the name Paul after his conversion.) Write out the account in your own words. Include what you think Saul was thinking before, during, and after the encounter.

Scripture doesn't tell us why Saul was blind for the next three days and we can assume that Saul didn't know if his sight would ever return. Scripture also doesn't tell us why he didn't eat or drink for three days. But we do know Saul's entire ideology had been dramatically overturned—he went from wanting to kill and persecute Christians to becoming one. And he was traveling with companions who shared his previous ideology.

God whispers to us in our pleasures, speaks in our conscience, but shouts in our pains: it is His megaphone to rouse a deaf world.
—C. S. Lewis (*Problem of Pain*, 81)

3. Try to imagine you are Saul. What would you be thinking during your three days of blindness? What do you think you would say, if anything, to your travel companions?

4. If you are a Christian, how did you come to faith in Jesus? If you aren't a Christian, what holds you back from believing in Jesus?

5. Your conversion experience may or may not have been outwardly dramatic like Paul's. Likely none of us have experienced literal blinding light, but some may have experienced 180-degree life change. What significant encounter(s) with God have you had since then?

6. Reread Galatians 1:13–14 (and also read Philippian 3:5–6 and Acts 8:3, if you have time). What used to make Paul credible before he was a believer? Why do you think Paul brought up who he used to be in an attempt to reestablish his credibility?

Why did God choose, prepare and then call Paul, the proud persecutor of His church? Was it because Paul was in some way, in any way, pleasing to God? No, it was simply because God "was pleased" to do so (v. 15). God set His loving grace on Paul not because he was worthy of it, but simply because God took delight or pleasure in doing so.
—Timothy Keller
(*Galatians*, 29)

I thank Christ Jesus our Lord, who has given me strength, that he considered me trustworthy, appointing me to his service. Even though I was once a blasphemer and a persecutor and a violent man, I was shown mercy because I acted in ignorance and unbelief. The grace of our Lord was poured out on me abundantly, along with the faith and love that are in Christ Jesus.
—the apostle Paul, in a letter to Timothy
(1 Timothy 1:12-14)

7. From the verses in question 6, how did Paul treat believers before his encounter with Christ? The severe persecution of Christians is still happening; in fact, it seems to be on the rise. Who currently is—like Saul—engaged in the severe persecution of Christians? (If you need help thinking of someone go to the Voice of the Martyrs website for ideas: www.persecution.com.) How would you feel if any of these people became believers? What would it take for you to believe their conversion was real?

I've told you these things to prepare you for rough times ahead. They are going to throw you out of the meeting places. There will even come a time when anyone who kills you will think he's doing God a favor. They will do these things because they never really understood the Father. I've told you these things so that when the time comes and they start in on you, you'll be well-warned and ready for them.
—John 16:1–3 MSG

8. How does Paul say some reacted to his conversion (Galatians 1:23–24)?

9. Galatians 1:15–16 reveals Paul's new mission—his calling by God's grace. He went from persecutor to preacher.

   When did God set Paul apart?

   What was God pleased to reveal?

   What was the purpose of all this?

Paul's conversion, then, reminds us of God's power to turn around the most unlikely people. We should never give up praying for those who seem impossible to reach, for salvation is of the Lord. Salvation is ultimately a miracle; it is a work of God.
—Thomas Schreiner (*Galatians*, 104)

10. Think of the people you care deeply about who don't know Jesus. How does Paul's conversion story encourage you?

11. Paul is now called to preach to the Gentiles. In what ways do you think his previous life as a well-trained religious Jew uniquely prepared him for this? Does this seem like an obvious calling for Paul? Why or why not?

DIGGING DEEPER

Several times in the early part of the Galatian letter, Paul emphasizes that he's not concerned with gaining people's admiration, only with living to please God regardless of what others think. What did Jesus teach in Luke 12:4–7 that Paul modeled in his ministry life? How could you apply this to your life?

12. Think through some of the unique parts of your life (both present and past—good and bad). How do these parts of your life uniquely prepare you to share the hope of Jesus with others? Is there a particular type of person you feel would be more receptive to your sharing as a result of your life experiences? Write a short prayer asking the Lord to give you opportunities to interact with and share Jesus with these types of people.

Jesus has called all of us to share the truth of the gospel with others (Matthew 28:18–20). This is commonly referred to as the Great Commission.

RETRAINING

DIGGING DEEPER

Like Jesus, Paul probably spent time alone in the desert before embarking on his formal ministry. Jesus spent forty days out there. Why do you think Jesus only needed forty days to prepare while Paul needed three years? Read Luke's account of Jesus's time of testing in the wilderness in Luke 4:1–13. Who do you think might have joined Paul as his "teacher"?

13. What does Paul say he did right after his conversion (vv. 16–17)? Many scholars believe Paul spent that time in the desert region outside of Damascus. How much time passed before he went to Jerusalem (v. 18)? What might he have done during this time?

14. Why did Paul say he went to Jerusalem (v. 18)? Did he meet any other apostles while he was there (v. 19)? Why might Paul be adamantly pointing out that he didn't spend any time with the other apostles?

Read Galatians 2:1–10.

WHAT'S THE REAL ISSUE?

15. Paul returns to Jerusalem fourteen years later with Barnabas and Titus. What do you learn about Titus in Galatians 2:3?

It is possible that Paul brought Titus, likely one of his early converts (cf. Titus 1:4) and a continual friend (2 Cor. 2:13), as a "test case." . . . This would force the Jewish believers of Jerusalem to admit that God was as much at work among, and through, Gentiles as Jews. . . . Paul's argument could not have been clearer: if God had chosen and was using this uncircumcised Gentile, then certainly circumcision was not required to join the people of God.

—Scot McKnight (*NIV Application Commentary*, 83)

16. What did Paul call the Judaizers? What did he say they were doing? (2:4)

Circumcision wasn't just a matter of keeping part of the law of Moses. It was a sign of membership in the covenant family of God, which some Jewish Christians (whom Paul calls false family members) said was also essential to the gospel. Over the centuries circumcision had become the marker of Israel's racial identity. Paul will insist in the course of this letter, however, that one does not need to become a part of a certain race to join God's family.

—N. T. Wright (*Galatians*, 14)

Paul expresses in verse 2 that he fearfully met privately with the apostles in Jerusalem to discuss the gospel message he had been preaching to the Gentiles. The stakes of this meeting were high. On the one side, Paul says the gospel is by faith in Jesus alone and is for all people. On the other side, the Judaizers say Gentiles could become Christians, but they needed to become Jewish first (symbolized by circumcision and keeping the Mosaic law). As Timothy Keller says, "If the Jerusalem apostles had sided with, or even merely tolerated, those who were teaching against Paul, this would have split the church in two. Neither side would have accepted the other fully, and would have questioned if the others were saved!" (*Galatians*, 39).

We must be exceedingly careful to make sure we understand someone's theology before branding anyone as a false brother or sister. To say works are a necessary evidence of salvation is not the same as saying that works are the ultimate basis of our salvation.

—Thomas Schreiner (*Galatians*, 132)

The Jerusalem apostles had been preaching Christ in Jerusalem to Jewish people and therefore had not had to work out the implications of what it would mean for a Gentile to convert to Christianity. They had a huge decision to make. Would they give in to their cultural biases as Jews and thereby create a catastrophic split in the church? Or would they rightly discern and understand that what Jesus did was for everyone—not just the Jewish people?

17. What does Paul say the Jerusalem apostles added to his message (v. 6)?

INDEPENDENT YET UNIFIED

This section helpfully illustrates the diversity within the unity of Christ's body. Different Christians can minister to different segments of humanity and to people in different regions. Nevertheless there must be unity in the message we proclaim.
—Thomas Constable
(*Notes*, 27)

18. Paul says that the pillars of the Jerusalem church extended the right hand of fellowship to him and Barnabas, recognizing that they had different callings (v. 9). What were their callings? (Note: if your translation uses the words *circumcised* and *uncircumcised*, the circumcised represent the Jewish people and the uncircumcised represent the Gentile people.)

    Paul and Barnabas were called to preach to the ___________________.

    James, Peter, and John were called to preach to the ________________.

19. Your practice this week relates to the one request the Jerusalem apostles made of Paul and Barnabas (v. 10). What was it and why is it a priority in the Christian life?

Crucified with Christ | LESSON 4

PRACTICE PRAYER

Lesson four centers on a tense interaction between Paul and Peter. Peter makes an unwise choice, which distracts and confuses the early believers. Paul boldly confronts him as a hypocrite who is compromising the gospel. Paul's words and actions feel like pretty heavy accusations toward another apostle.

As we've seen throughout this study, Paul's main focus is grace-centered preaching and establishing the truth of the gospel. One of the added benefits of this pursuit is unity. Paul knew that a disagreement on the fundamentals would lead to a destructive fissure in the church and could leave followers wondering whose message was theologically correct.

This is still an issue today. There are so many different denominations and churches that it's impossible to keep track of them all. How do we determine who's right? Where exactly do we draw the line? Paul would tell us to draw the line at the essentials. Everything else is preference. But we really like our preferences, don't we?

This week we are going to direct our hearts toward unity through intentionally praying for a Christian church other than the one we regularly attend.

You probably drive by multiple churches in the course of daily life. Choose one of them and then go online to learn more about them. Start with their statement of faith. If you learn that they don't adhere to the essentials of the gospel—like maybe they don't believe Jesus is the Son of God—then please choose another church. While we are to be graciously disposed and loving toward all, this activity is to build unity within the Christian body. Beyond the essentials, resist the temptation to judge them.

Your next step will be to gather information so you can pray for them (for example, the senior pastor's name, types of programming they offer, recent preaching topics). Spend three to five minutes each day this

OPTIONAL

Memorize Galatians 2:20

I have been crucified with Christ and I no longer live, but Christ lives in me. The life I now live in the body, I live by faith in the Son of God, who loved me and gave himself for me.

week intentionally praying for that church and their leaders. Here are a few suggestions:

Ask the Lord to protect and encourage them.
Ask the Lord to make their ministry effective and fruitful.
Pray for their upcoming events or sermons.

We hope that when you pray for this other church you will realize that more unifies us than divides us. Unity was of high value to Jesus. In John 17:20–21, he prayed, "I am praying not only for these disciples but also for *all who will ever believe in me* through their message. *I pray that they will all be one*" (paraphrase and emphasis ours). Did you catch that? He prayed for you to be one with other believers. We pray this small activity moves us in that direction.

After completing the exercise, reflect on your experience by answering these questions:

- Did you have any initial areas of resistance in your heart to this activity (competitive, judgmental, etc.)?

- As you prayed, what changes did you notice in your heart-attitude toward this church?

- As you prayed, did you notice any changes in your heart toward your own church? If so, in what ways? If not, why not?

This section wraps up Paul's defense as one sent by Jesus and not other people. From here he transitions to the core of his salvation-by-grace-alone-in-Christ-alone theology. You'll start to see this transition in the second half of the lesson.

Read Galatians 2:11–14.

THE SIN OF A LEADER

1. Glance back at Galatians 1:18–19 and 2:7–9.

   Who was Peter?

   What do these verses say about Paul's interactions with Peter?

   What happens in 2:11?

2. According to verse 12, what was Peter doing and why? Who was Peter afraid of? What was the impact (v. 13)?

DIGGING DEEPER

God orchestrated an elaborate set of circumstances to show Peter that he did not need to obey the Jewish food laws, that he was free to eat with Gentiles, and that the Gentiles could become Christians without becoming Jews first. To understand what God did, study Acts 10 and 11. In light of these experiences, are you surprised at Peter's reluctance to eat with Gentiles, requiring Paul's rebuke? What do you learn about all of us from this situation?

3. Paul confronts Peter publicly with what appears to be some scathing words (v. 14). Rewrite what Paul says in your own words.

4. Has anyone ever publicly opposed you to your face? How did it make you feel?

5. Compare Matthew 18:15–17 and 1 Timothy 5:20. (Note that 1 Timothy is directed to church leaders.) According to these passages, do you think Paul handled this conflict well? Was Paul justified in making this rebuke in public? Why or why not?

6. Paul says Peter was forcing (NIV) or compelling (NASB) Gentiles to live like Jews. How was Peter doing this?

7. Peter was exhibiting legalism, an overemphasis on rule-following. He was compelling the Gentile believers to follow Jewish customs in order to prove their right standing with God. What are some ways churches are legalistic today? If you have personally encountered legalism, share your experience with the group. (No names, please.)

There are varying degrees of legalism. Blatant legalism says you must add something to faith to be saved. Subtle legalism is harder to spot because there's a fine line between motivation and legalistic pressure. For example, we all believe we should spend time with God through reading Scripture and praying—but what's our motivation? Are we trying to earn something from God or appease him (or someone else)? If so, we've probably fallen into legalistic behavior. If our motivation is out of love and a desire for a deeper relationship, then we are on the right track.

8. Peter was an apostle—a man chosen by Jesus to lead the early church—yet he still sinned. What kind of expectations do you have for church leaders? When do you think sin necessitates private rebuke, public rebuke, or removal from ministry?

Conflict among Christians almost always makes Jesus look bad and must be entered into with caution. Back in the nineties, a woman in my church accused me of "false teaching" when actually the point of disagreement was a gray issue that professors in our seminary agree to disagree over. For over a year she attempted to destroy my reputation and my ministry. Ultimately I was exonerated and the result was a book to help other leaders who find themselves in similar situations, but the conflict took a toll on my life and the life of the church. The warning: Don't enter into conflict lightly or over preferences. Make sure it's an issue worth debating. In Paul's case it was, but in many conflicts in the church, it isn't. —Sue

The reality is everyone is vulnerable to sin. Take a moment to pray for the leaders of your church (and other ministries) to be strengthened in their dependence upon the Lord and protected from stumbling into sin—especially sins that could threaten the gospel.

9. Read Acts 15:7–11. Assuming this passage was written after Paul confronted Peter, how did Peter change?

As evidenced by other parts of the New Testament, Peter repented and was restored to leadership in the Christian church. Paul was strong in his confrontation with Peter. But if you look closely you'll notice that while Peter and the Judaizers both distorted the gospel, Paul never called Peter a "false brother" as he did with the Judaizers. This may be because Peter, a true brother, had just lost his way and was acting hypocritically.

Read Galatians 2:15–16.

JUSTIFIED

In this passage, Paul shifts from direct confrontation to theological debate.

Unsaved Jews regarded Gentiles as "sinners." Paul ironically referred to them this way here, since Peter was discriminating against them by behaving as he had.
—Thomas Constable (*Notes*, 29)

10. Galatians 2:16 is a key verse in the book. Count the number of times the words *justified*, *works of the law*, and *faith in (Jesus) Christ* are used. What do you think Paul is communicating by this repetition?

Note: Two actions happen when we are justified. The first is a subtraction—the removal of our sins. The second is an addition—the gift of Christ's righteousness. God removes our guilt and the penalty for our sin by giving us Christ's innocence.

> **Justified**—This basic forensic Greek word describes a judge declaring an accused person not guilty and therefore innocent before the law. Throughout Scripture it refers to God's declaring a sinner not guilty and fully righteous before Him by imputing to him the divine righteousness of Christ and imputing the person's sin to the sinless Savior for punishment. (MacArthur, *Galatians*, 26)

11. Read 2 Corinthians 5:21. According to this verse, Jesus, the one "who had no sin," was made what by God?

    Why?

    Reread the definition of *justified* in the note above. How does this verse support the fact that our sin is not only taken away, but we are given the very righteousness of Christ?

Different people land on different verses as the "key verse" in Galatians. Several seem to be good candidates. My favorites are Galatians 2:16, 5:1, and 5:16. —Jodie

One of my favorite online Bible sites is biblegateway.com. They have lots of translations and there's even a feature that will let you compare them side by side. —Jodie

At bible.org, you can access the NET Bible. One of its fabulous features is its gender accuracy. For example, many older translations say "brothers" when it more accurately would read, "brothers and sisters." For women who have been told that Christianity does not value women, the inclusive language sets the record straight. You can also read quality blogs there, including mine. —Sue

12. Under the "Jesus" figure below, write down some words that describe Jesus and his righteousness. Next, put your name above the other figure and write down some words that describe your sins. Now cross out Jesus's name and write your own in its place. Cross out your name and write "Jesus" in its place. Do you believe Jesus's righteousness is really associated with you now? Why or why not?

The chart doesn't tell the whole story though. Through Jesus's death on the cross he paid for all our sins. This means that any words you wrote under the figure that now bears the name "Jesus" no longer apply. To symbolize this, draw a big cross over this figure, and then do a little happy dance.

This exchange is often referred to as imputed righteousness. God took our sin and gave it to Jesus and then he took Jesus's righteousness and gave it to us. This great exchange means that in the sight of God we are as righteous and acceptable as Jesus Christ. All that is required is our faith.

Read Galatians 2:17–19.

DEAD TO LAW

This set of verses can be tricky. It's easy to get lost in what Paul is saying. Different translations hit on different nuances in the text; for this passage we found the New Living Translation helpful. However, if you have time, we recommend reading a few different translations to assist you in your study and understanding of these verses.

Paul refuted the charge of the Judaizers that justification by faith led to lawless behavior. . . . If a Christian puts himself or herself back under the law, the law will show him or her to be a sinner, since no one can keep the law perfectly.
—Thomas Constable
(*Notes*, 31)

13. According to this passage and Romans 6:15–18, does freedom from the law mean Christ advocates sin?

14. Look up the word *condemned* in a dictionary and write a brief definition below. Paul says the law condemns. According to James 2:10, why is this true?

Condemnation and conviction are very different. Condemnation attacks our worth and value and tells us we've fallen too far to be redeemed. This is, of course, a huge lie that comes from either the enemy or the "mean voice" in our own head. Conviction, on the other hand, comes from the Holy Spirit and leads us lovingly toward repentance. It does not attack our worth or value. Always listen to the promptings that lead you to God and tell the other ones to get lost.

15. Have you ever felt "condemned" for something? What happened? And how did it feel?

16. Have you ever felt God convict you of something? Did God's conviction feel different than condemnation? If so, how?

I rejected the church for a time because I found so little grace there. I returned because I found grace nowhere else.
—Philip Yancey (*What's So Amazing*, 16)

17. How did Paul die to the law (v. 19)? What did this enable him to do? What does this imply for anyone choosing to stay under the law?

18. What do you think it means to live for God (v. 19; see also Matthew 22:37–40 and Galatians 5:13–14)? Where are you struggling to "live for God" in your life right now? Why do you think this is a struggle?

Read Galatians 2:20–21.

CRUCIFIED WITH CHRIST

Galatians 2:20–21 sums up the entire message of Galatians in a nutshell. These verses are full of truths that we could (and perhaps should) meditate on for a lifetime. Before we dive into them, let's remember the big picture.

The Judaizers were teaching that believers needed to come through Judaism (via the law) to be truly saved. Essentially they believed Jesus didn't abolish the law, but was an addition to the law. Thus, according to them, one needed both Jesus and the law.

This frustrated Paul. The Judaizers' "gospel" was really no gospel at all. Once you add anything to salvation through faith in Jesus alone, you are essentially saying Jesus alone is insufficient. This does more than water down the gospel; it destroys it.

Paul uses the powerful metaphor of death (crucifixion) and resurrection (life) in these verses to make his point clear: Christ's crucifixion puts to death the old (who we were) and his resurrection raises to life the new (who we are in Christ now).

This means that anyone who belongs to Christ has become a new person. The old life is gone; a new life has begun!
—2 Corinthians 5:17 NLT

19. Paul says he has been crucified with Christ (v. 20). What do you think this means? (Refer back to question 12 to help you visually think about this concept.) In what way have you been crucified with Christ?

DIGGING DEEPER

Paul wrote a marvelous further explanation of the resources available to Christians because of the reality that God sees us united with Christ in his death and resurrection. Read Romans 6 and then write out the truths you discover there. How do you feel about your new life in Christ after wringing out these truths? What is one thing you need to change in your life in light of these truths?

20. According to verse 20, what is the result of being crucified with Christ? Does Christ live in you? Have you noticed any difference in the way you live now as a Christian versus how you lived before you became a believer (or how you might now live if you had not accepted Christ)?

When a person trusts Christ, God identifies him or her with Christ, not only in the present and future, but also in the past. The believer did what Christ did. When Christ died, I died. When Christ arose from the grave, I arose to newness of life. My old self-centered life died when I died with Christ.
—Thomas Constable (*Notes*, 33)

21. Jot down some of the key words, phrases, and ideas from Galatians 2:15–21. In as few words as possible, what do you think is Paul's main point in these verses?

Declared Righteous

LESSON 5

OPTIONAL

Memorize Ephesians 2:8–9

For it is by grace you have been saved, through faith—and this is not from yourselves, it is the gift of God—not by works, so that no one can boast.

PRACTICE ✿ JOURNALING

Do you remember the moment you first believed in Jesus? Do you remember what it was like to have the Holy Spirit awaken your soul in this new way? What about all the answered prayers you've experienced? Remember that time that car should have hit you, but it didn't? Or that time healing came?

Chances are you remember some of these experiences, but it's likely time has dulled others. Journaling can help jog our memories—often as we begin writing, memories return.

This week we are going to journal to help us recall ways God has providentially intervened in our lives.

This journaling activity is to help you remember, not to make you stressed. So journal however is best for you. Some people like to use complete sentences with proper punctuation and others like to capture just words and phrases. Some people doodle and draw instead of using words.

Try to set aside about thirty minutes this week to complete this activity. Consider the two sets of journaling prompts below—your conversion story and significant answered prayers. Spend a few minutes brainstorming each one and then choose the one you want to explore through journaling. Make the effort to complete this activity. It will be well worth your time.

You don't have to share your discoveries with anyone, but we hope you will. We've found the Lord uses others' stories of conversion, answered prayers, and provision to encourage our often-weary hearts. Maybe your story will be just the encouragement someone needs. Remember, our God is living and active—sometimes we just forget.

Option A: Conversion Memories

- What is your earliest memory of God?
- What happened to make you believe in Jesus for the first time? Do you remember where you were? What led up to this moment? Describe the place, words, people, sounds, smells, and feelings. (If you were a very young child when you first believed in Jesus, describe a moment when you had a significant encounter with God—maybe a time when you first became serious about your faith.)
- How did your life change after that moment?

Option B: Answered Prayers

- What is the earliest answered prayer you can remember?
- What is your most recent answered prayer?
- What are some other answered prayers you've experienced (think of loved ones; jobs; big decisions; protection; healings—emotional, relational, or physical; etc.)?
- Choose one of the answered prayers above and describe in detail what happened. What were you specifically praying for? Who else was praying? How long had you been praying? What was happening the moment you realized the prayer was answered? Where were you? What were you doing? How did you feel in that moment? How did you know it was God? What changed as a result of this answered prayer?

After completing the exercise, reflect on your experience by answering these questions:

- What surprised you, if anything, about doing this journaling activity?

- Do you ever share the story you wrote about with others? Why or why not? If not, consider sharing it with someone this week.

Paul pleads with the Galatians to remember. He asks them to recall their early experience with Christ—to reflect back on what really happened. He tells them they would be foolish to forget.

But Paul also knows experiences alone can't be the foundation of our faith. Faith experiences must be bolstered by the truth. So after Paul asks them to remember their experiences, he reminds them of some essential truths.

DIGGING DEEPER

Memorize Ephesians 2:4–9.

Read Galatians 3:1–5.

REMEMBER YOUR EXPERIENCES

In the verses prior to this section, Paul has outlined that our righteousness comes from faith alone in Christ alone.

1. Paul peppers the Galatians with at least five questions (depending on your translation). Fill in the chart below summarizing each verse's main question in your own words. If there is an obvious answer to the question, write it in the second box. We've done verse 4 for you as an example.

Verse	Question	Answer
3:1		
3:2		
3:3		
3:4	Did you go through all of this for nothing?	Paul doesn't know the answer yet. He is hopeful, but the Galatians will ultimately have to choose.
3:5		

The Holy Spirit takes up residence within us the moment we believe that Jesus's death paid the penalty for our sin and that his resurrection brings us new life. There are no other hoops to jump through. Paul's current focus is our understanding of salvation through faith alone, but soon he will turn the corner to help us start living in the power of the Spirit. After all, the Spirit didn't move in to leave us unchanged; he moved in to empower us to live our lives in a new way. If you feel stalled or defeated, don't lose hope. As a believer, the Holy Spirit resides in you. Ask God to help you understand how to live in the Spirit.

2. In verse 2 Paul asks how they received the Holy Spirit. Have you received the Spirit? How do you know? (See also John 14:16–17; Romans 8:9; and Ephesians 1:13.)

IMPORTANT REMINDERS FROM SCRIPTURE

In Galatians 3:6–14, Paul quotes numerous Old Testament verses. The Judaizers had probably misused Old Testament Scriptures in their arguments which Paul is now refuting. By quoting these passages, Paul is showing the Galatians how God always intended to include the Gentiles and always intended salvation to be by faith.

Much of what Paul discusses in these verses are truths we have worked through and discussed in previous lessons. Repetition is a great learning tool, though. So let's interact with these truths again but in a different way.

On the next page, we've printed the passage in two different translations. Grab a few colored pens or pencils (if you want) and get ready to interact with the text. To begin, read both versions aloud.

A note on translations: A wide spectrum of translations exists: from word-for-word, to thought-for-thought, to paraphrase. Word-for-word is great for serious Scripture study as it aims to translate each word as accurately as possible. The downside is that it can be harder to read and we may find ourselves getting lost in the individual words and unable to capture the larger meaning of the text. Thought-for-thought aims to translate each thought. This makes it easier to read. The downside is we can miss important nuances of the text. Paraphrase translates the text into modern language and aims to communicate the story of Scripture. Paraphrase is great for devotional-type reading, but we may sacrifice accuracy.

We like to use many different translations when we study. We primarily read the NIV 2011, a thought-for-thought translation. When we study we often consult the New American Standard Bible (NASB, a word-for-word), the New Living Translation (NLT, a thought-for-thought) and The Message (MSG, a paraphrase). Each Bible is useful for different purposes.

Read Galatians 3:6–14.

New Living Translation (NLT)

6 In the same way, "Abraham
believed God, and God counted
him as righteous because of his
faith." 7 The real children of
Abraham, then, are those who
put their faith in God.

8 What's more, the Scriptures
looked forward to this time when
God would make the Gentiles
right in his sight because of their
faith. God proclaimed this good
news to Abraham long ago when
he said, "All nations will be
blessed through you." 9 So all who
put their faith in Christ share the
same blessing Abraham received
because of his faith.

10 But those who depend on the
law to make them right with
God are under his curse, for
the Scriptures say, "Cursed is
everyone who does not observe
and obey all the commands that
are written in God's Book of the
law." 11 So it is clear that no one
can be made right with God by
trying to keep the law. For the
Scriptures say, "It is through
faith that a righteous person
has life." 12 This way of faith is
very different from the way of
law, which says, "It is through
obeying the law that a person has
life."

13 But Christ has rescued us from
the curse pronounced by the
law. When he was hung on the
cross, he took upon himself the
curse for our wrongdoing. For
it is written in the Scriptures,
"Cursed is everyone who is
hung on a tree." 14 Through
Christ Jesus, God has blessed the
Gentiles with the same blessing
he promised to Abraham, so
that we who are believers might
receive the promised Holy Spirit
through faith.

New International Version (NIV)

6 So also Abraham "believed
God, and it was credited to him
as righteousness." 7 Understand,
then, that those who have faith
are children of Abraham.

8 Scripture foresaw that God
would justify the Gentiles by
faith, and announced the gospel
in advance to Abraham: "All
nations will be blessed through
you." 9 So those who rely on faith
are blessed along with Abraham,
the man of faith.

10 For all who rely on the works
of the law are under a curse, as it
is written: "Cursed is everyone
who does not continue to do
everything written in the Book
of the Law." 11 Clearly no one who
relies on the law is justified before
God, because "the righteous will
live by faith." 12 The law is not
based on faith; on the contrary, it
says, "The person who does these
things will live by them."

13 Christ redeemed us from the
curse of the law by becoming
a curse for us, for it is written:
"Cursed is everyone who is hung
on a pole." 14 He redeemed us
in order that the blessing given
to Abraham might come to the
Gentiles through Christ Jesus, so
that by faith we might receive the
promise of the Spirit.

OBSERVATION

3. Note any repeated or key words or phrases that stand out to you. Jot them in the right margin of the passage.

With the Mosaic law came requirements, rules, regulations. With those exacting demands came galling expectations, which fueled the Pharisees' fire. By adding to the laws, the Pharisees not only lengthened the list, they intensified everyone's guilt and shame. Obsessed with duty, external conduct, and a constant focusing only on right and wrong (especially in others' lives), they promoted a system so demanding there was no room left for joy. This led to harsh, judgmental, even prejudicial announcements as the religious system they promoted degenerated into external performance rather than internal authenticity. Obedience became a matter of grim compulsion instead of a joyous overflow prompted by love.
—Charles Swindoll
(*Grace Awakening*, 7)

4. Read through the passages a second time and mark the following words: *Abraham*, *law*, *faith*, and *curse*. We recommend you use a different color and/or symbol (underline, circle, triangle, cloud, square, etc.) for each word.

5. List all the people in the passage.

6. List all the actions taking place in the passage.

7. List the words or phrases Paul associates with Abraham and the words or phrases he associates with the law.

Abraham	**Law**

8. Write down any additional observations.

> The words "it was credited to him" were written not for him alone, but also for us, to whom God will credit righteousness—for us who believe in him who raised Jesus our Lord from the dead. He was delivered over to death for our sins and was raised to life for our justification.
> —Romans 4:23-25

INTERPRETATION

9. Flip back to lesson 1, questions 1 and 2 (pages 15–16), where we first discussed the Abrahamic covenant. How does this passage support what you learned in lesson 1 about the Abrahamic covenant?

10. Flip back to lesson 4 questions 12 and 13 (pages 52–53), where we learned Christians are declared righteous. How does verse 13 support the truth you discovered in those questions?

11. What members of the Trinity are mentioned in this passage? Why do you think this is significant? Did you notice any distinctions in their roles?

12. In your own words, what do you think is the main point Paul is trying to communicate?

DIGGING DEEPER

In Paul's letter to the church in Rome he also explains that Abraham was not justified by works but by his faith in God's promises. Read Romans 4 and create an argument that you would make to the Judaizers as to why salvation is by faith alone in Christ alone rather than by works of the law.

13. Imagine you are the original recipient of this letter—being corrected by Paul for accepting the teachings of the Judaizers. How would you hear these words? What would stand out to you?

APPLICATION

In this application section, you may not have answers for every question or even feel you need to answer every question, and that's okay. These questions are to help you wrestle with and think through the truths of this passage. Spend some time exploring the areas you struggle to believe are true for you.

14. Do you think you're included in this passage? If so, where or in what ways?

15. Do you ever feel like you are living under a "curse"? If so, in what way and why?

DIGGING DEEPER

Still think you can (or should) earn your way to righteousness? Check out James 2:10 and Romans 3:20.

16. Do you feel you need to do certain things to be right with God? If so, what? Why do you think you do this?

17. Do you believe you are righteous? Why or why not?

Ponder the achievement of God. He doesn't condone our sin; nor does he compromise his standard. He doesn't ignore our rebellion; nor does he relax his demands. Rather than dismiss our sin he assumes our sin and, incredibly, sentences himself. God's holiness is honored. Our sin is punished. And we are redeemed. God is still God. The wages of sin is still death. And we are made perfect. . . . And what should be your response?

—Max Lucado (*In the Grip of Grace*, 75)

18. Do you believe you can lose (or ever have lost) your righteous standing? Why or why not?

19. Is there a truth you need to believe regarding this passage? Or is there an untruth you need to let go of?

20. Is there something practical you should do this week because of the information you discovered in this passage? If so, what is it? Consider sharing this with friends for accountability.

The Law—Then and Now | LESSON 6

PRACTICE ✻ STUDY

Paul had been pressing in hard on the Galatians. Frustrated because they had added the law back in, he called them foolish as he pointed out their inconsistencies. Why would they start with a grace-based faith and then think they needed to add works to be acceptable? That just didn't make sense to Paul's understanding of the grace and freedom Jesus offers.

At this point he anticipated the million-dollar question from the Galatians: "So, why did God even bother giving the law if he didn't expect us to live by it?"

It's a great question. Why was the law given? How do we relate to the law today? Do we toss it aside? Do we try to live by it? Do we only have to live by certain parts of it?

To answer these we need to go on a few excursions. First, we'll see what Jesus said about the law. Next, we'll discover that neither Paul nor Jesus advocated for lawless living; rather, they both led us to a new way—the law of love. A law that flows from the inside out, not a law imposed externally as a measurable action.

Set aside time each day to intentionally and diligently do your study.

This week we have a lot to learn, so our practice will be our lesson. This practice will help us love God with our minds (Matthew 22:37).

You've probably caught on that we're pretty passionate about all of us becoming diligent Bible students—especially because knowing the truth brings freedom. Jesus said: "If you hold to my teaching, you are really my disciples. Then you will know the truth, and the truth will set you free" (John 8:31–32). We find truth in Scripture. And, unfortunately, when we don't understand God's truth, we are easily enslaved by error.

Lesson 6 contains an important link in understanding truth—especially concerning the law. A misapplied verse can lead us to believe we need to earn God's favor through our works, or on the flip side, that we are experiencing struggles and trials because we have neglected our works.

OPTIONAL

Memorize
Romans 3:19–20

Now we know that whatever the law says, it says to those who are under the law, so that every mouth may be silenced and the whole world held accountable to God. Therefore no one will be declared righteous in God's sight by the works of the law; rather, through the law we become conscious of our sin.

"Teacher, which is the greatest commandment in the Law?"

Jesus replied: "'Love the Lord your God with all your heart and with all your soul and with all your mind.' This is the first and greatest commandment. And the second is like it: 'Love your neighbor as yourself.'"

—Matthew 22:36–39

We see it happen all the time. For example, recently someone said, "I just don't know why this is happening because I've been so faithful to God lately." This is living life under "law"—checking a box with God and expecting him to do something in return. It doesn't work this way. Does that mean we shouldn't seek to live obedient and God-honoring lives? No. It just means we need to check our heart—and we need to make sure we correctly understand Scripture.

Without proper interpretation we can quickly find ourselves in the same territory as the Galatians—adding works to our faith for all the wrong reasons. We study all of God's Word so we know how to properly interpret verses and won't take them out of context or misapply them.

Freedom comes when we know the truth. And freedom is a pretty good payoff for diligent Bible study.

After completing the exercise, reflect on your experience by answering these questions:

- Were you able to make intentional time for your study this week? Why or why not?

- How did intentionality in your study help you love God with your heart, soul, and mind (Matthew 22:37)?

- What freedom did you feel as a result of learning truth this week?

Before I (Sue) accepted Christ as my Savior, my husband and I attended a church embroiled in legalism. We were a floundering young couple desperately looking for a community that emphasized strong family values and right living. But soon, I began to feel the squeeze of a never-ending list of legalistic rules and regulations. They suffocated us individually and put a strain on our marriage.

I remember the day we left that church for another that focused on God's grace and goodness. I felt like a bird freed from a cage—finally I could fly. That was forty years ago. Today we both enjoy a vibrant, passionate relationship with the Lord. We've thrived as individuals and our marriage is strong. Every day I thank God for his grace and his freedom from legalism. In order for any of us to live in that grace and freedom, we must understand the purpose of the law.

So, then, what was the purpose of the law? If it doesn't bring us life, why did God create it? What do we do with it now? And more importantly, how do we live in a relationship with God that's vibrant, growing, and full of freedom and joy? We will find answers in this lesson.

Read Galatians 3:15–25.

LAW AS TEMPORARY

Before we begin this section, we need a clear understanding of what Paul means by the term *law*. It's often used to mean different things. Sometimes people use the term *law* to specifically refer to the Ten Commandments and other times to refer to the entire Old Testament. When Paul uses the term *law* he specifically refers to the Mosaic covenant between God and the nation of Israel, instituted on Mount Sinai and ending at the death of Jesus Christ.

1. How does Paul answer the question, "Why, then, was the law given?" (3:19)?

The Mosaic law is composed of 613 commands, which can be divided into three categories. First the moral law, usually considered the Ten Commandments (Exodus 20:1–17). Second the civil law, which gave Israel guidelines for how they were to interact with one another and with foreigners. Third the ceremonial law, which instructed Israel on proper worship and relationship with God. (The civil and ceremonial laws are found in Exodus 21 and in all of Leviticus.) Interestingly, circumcision, one of the main points Paul is contending against, is instituted with Abraham in Genesis 17—over 400 years before the Mosaic law. Circumcision was a central issue because it showed who belonged to the nation of Israel, and who was and was not under the law.

2. Paul says the law was "given alongside the promise" (3:19 NLT). Based on Galatians 3:15–18, what promise is Paul referring to?

Only when I had grown exhausted with the doing did I begin to consider the idea that maybe, just maybe, God had something more in mind for me, something more meaningful, more satisfying than checking items off of a spiritual to-do list.
—Jan Winebrenner
(*Intimate Faith*, 219)

3. How long was the law to last (3:19)? Has this "seed" or "child" (NLT) come (see 3:16)? What does this mean about the law?

LAW AS SIN DEFINER

4. What does the law show us (3:20–22)? According to Romans 7:7–8, what else does the law do?

5. If you saw this sign posted above a hole in a wall, what would you be tempted to do?

If the sign wasn't there, what would you be likely to do?

6. Recall a time when someone told you not to do something that you had not even considered doing. What happened? How did you react to their direction?

LAW AS GUARDIAN

In verse 24 the NIV and NLT use the word "guardian" and the NASB uses the word "tutor." The law served as a "tutor" (NASB). The word *paidagōgos* is difficult to render into English since there is no exact parallel to this position in modern society . . . The pedagogue here was . . . a slave to whom a son was committed from age six or seven to puberty. These slaves were severe disciplinarians and were charged with guarding the children from the evils of society and giving them moral training. . . . (The law) was the disciplinarian until Christ came.
—Donald Campbell ("Galatians," 600)

7. In Galatians 3:24–25, Paul describes the law as a guardian or tutor. Read the sidebar explanation for this term. In what ways do you think the law served as a tutor for the Israelites?

8. Think back to when you were a child. Who were some of the adults who guarded you and supplied moral training? What were some of the important lessons you learned? How did these lessons impact the person you became?

LAW AS HOLY

9. Read Romans 7:12 and Deuteronomy 4:8. What do these verses say about the law? What does this reveal about God?

Keep in mind that the law was never flawed. Only people are flawed. And to this end, the law reveals something else very important.

LAW AS REVEALER

10. Read Romans 3:20–23. How are we made right with God?

Is this true for Jewish people, Gentiles (which includes us), or both?

Who needs this truth? Why?

One of the most serious problems facing the orthodox Christian church today is the problem of legalism. One of the most serious problems facing the church in Paul's day was the problem of legalism. In every day it is the same. Legalism wrenches the joy of the Lord from the Christian believer, and with the joy of the Lord goes his power for vital worship and vibrant service. Nothing is left but cramped, somber, dull, and listless profession. The truth is betrayed, and the glorious name of the Lord becomes a synonym for a gloomy kill-joy. The Christian under law is a miserable parody of the real thing.
—Lewis Johnson ("Paralysis of Legalism," 109)

The law reveals our need for a Savior. Speaking of Jesus, let's take a look at what he had to say about the law.

JESUS AND THE LAW

11. Read Matthew 5:17–20. What did Jesus not come to do, and what did he come to do (v. 17)? What do you think he means when he says he fulfills the law?

When Jesus said "your righteousness must surpass that of the Pharisees and teachers of the law," he was teaching that we must be exceedingly righteous—which we know we can't do on our own. Jesus is also being slightly ironic—because he is getting ready to pull the righteous rug out from under the Pharisees and show that their actions were far from righteous. They had become so concerned with external conformity that they neglected the heart. Jesus raised the bar beyond reach when he showed us our actions must come out of our internal transformation—not our external conformation.

12. What does Jesus say happens if you break even one of the commandments (v. 19; see also James 2:10)? Who must you exceed in righteousness to enter the kingdom of heaven (Matthew 5:20)?

The law was never intended to be a means to salvation because, as we've seen, it was impossible to keep perfectly. And because we could not keep the law we were "cursed" (Galatians 3:10). Yet Jesus, in his death and resurrection, was able to fulfill the law and take the curse away (v. 13). To prove his point, Jesus continued his teaching by showing the true intent of the law.

13. Read Matthew 5:21–22. The sixth commandment says, "You shall not murder" (Exodus 20:13). How did Jesus move this command from external to internal? Have you been able to perfectly keep this command? Share any related struggles or victories.

14. Read Matthew 5:27–28. The seventh commandment says, "You shall not commit adultery" (Exodus 20:14). How did Jesus move this command from external to internal? Have you been able to perfectly keep this command? Share any related struggles or victories.

15. Later, Jesus spoke scathing words describing the Pharisees and teachers of the law. Rewrite Matthew 23:25–26 in your own words. What do you think Jesus was saying?

16. The Pharisees and teachers of the law were mainly concerned with external performance. Today we call this legalism. It occurs any time a rule or regulation is imposed on our relationship with God as a means for earning righteousness, favor, or blessing, or as a way to ensure we avoid sin or someone's interpretation of sin. What are some rules and regulations Christians impose on others today? Have you had any personal experience with legalism? If so, what happened?

17. Jesus sums up the law in Matthew 22:37–40. Write this summary in your own words.

Jesus's summary of the law was clearly easier to remember than 613 commands—but it required thinking. Those who wanted to obey God could no longer mindlessly follow a list of rules; instead, they had to examine their hearts.

18. Which law do you think is harder to keep, the Mosaic law or Jesus's summary of the law? Why?

The original Greek word, *huios*, in verse 26 is often translated as "children," but is best translated as the masculine word "sons." However, this does not mean women were not equally considered God's children. Paul indicates this by saying within almost the same breath, "There is neither . . . male and female, for you are all one in Christ" (v. 28). Paul intentionally chose the masculine word "sons" because he understood that the original audience considered sons to be of the greatest value to a father. A close reading of this passage shows that Paul is actually honoring and elevating the worth of women as he takes the common societal belief about men and applies it to women.

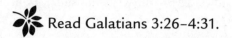

Read Galatians 3:26–4:31.

ONE IN CHRIST

Paul makes four theological arguments for why the Galatians should reject the teachings of the Judaizers. He roots his first reason in the Old Testament Scriptures (Galatians 3:6–14). We studied this defense in a previous lesson. His second argument comes out of the law and its purposes (Galatians 3:15–25). We studied this in the beginning of this lesson. His third reason is based on the fact that we are adopted as God's children into one unified family (Galatians 3:26–4:20). And his last reason comes from an illustration of Abraham and his two sons (Galatians 4:21–31). Let's quickly look at these last two reasons.

As we enter into Paul's third theological argument, remember the Judaizers were preaching that salvation was available for some and not for others. So Paul begins with the reminder that we, as God's children, should be unified.

19. Why do you think Paul brings in slavery and gender (3:28–29)?

This must have been glorious news for the Galatian Christians, for in their society slaves were considered to be only pieces of property; women were kept confined and disrespected; and Gentiles were constantly sneered at by the Jews. The Pharisee would pray each morning, "I thank Thee, God, that I am a Jew, not a Gentile; a man, not a woman; and a freeman, and not a slave." Yet all these distinctions are removed "in Christ."

—Warren Wiersbe (*Bible Exposition Commentary*, 704)

20. Where do you see yourself in this verse (gender, race, status)? Have you ever felt excluded because of who you are? How does this verse encourage you?

21. If we belong to Christ, what does 3:29 reveal about our heritage? Why is this important?

WHO WE WERE AND WHO WE ARE

In Galatians 4:1–3, Paul uses the illustration of children not yet old enough to legally inherit an estate to help us understand our life before Christ.

Scholars differ on what Paul meant by the phrase, "basic spiritual principles of this world" in verse 3 (NLT). In context, it seems Paul refers to one's philosophical and religious beliefs before Christ. For the Jews it's the Mosaic law (4:5). For Gentiles it's their previous worship of false gods (4:8). Paul is saying that before Christ we were all in bondage to something.

23. Since we are God's children, what else does that make us (4:7)? What will we inherit (3:29; see also Genesis 12:2–3)? What, ultimately, do we inherit?

DIGGING DEEPER

According to Romans 8:2 how should the indwelling Spirit impact our lives? What other ways should the Spirit's indwelling impact our lives? To answer this, look up one or more of the following verses: John 14:16–17, John 16:12–15, Acts 1:8, Romans 8:26–27, Romans 15:13, 1 Corinthians 2:13–14, and Galatians 5:16.

CHILDREN OF THE PROMISE

In the last section of Paul's theological defense against the Judaizers, Paul turns to the story of Abraham's two children. One child, Ishmael, was the illegitimate child of the slave woman Hagar (Genesis 16:1–4, 15), and one child, Isaac, was the child of the promise born to his wife Sarah (Genesis 21:1–5). It's hard to say why Paul makes this his last theological argument. It can seem out of place and confusing. Possibly the Judaizers were using the story of Abraham's two sons to try to prove that the Gentiles were akin to the illegitimate child Ishmael. Paul turns this thinking on its head and proves the exact opposite is true.

Try not to get lost in the details of this story. Paul uses this factual story to teach an allegorical lesson.

24. Write out all the contrasts between Sarah's child and Hagar's child found in Galatians 4:21–31. As Christians, which child are we?

We've officially wrapped up the theology section of Galatians. As we move into the practical application section of the letter, hold on to this theology. It establishes a foundation that will help us understand Paul's coming practical teaching throughout the rest of Galatians.

These last three lessons concern the everyday outworking of living in our freedom. As we've seen, we've been released from the law. But, as we will learn, we've also been released to living an abundant life in the Spirit. So, let's get to it—abundant life is waiting for each of us.

For Freedom | LESSON 7

PRACTICE ✤ LOVE YOUR NEIGHBOR

Love your neighbor as yourself.

We've all heard it. Jesus said it and Paul restated it in Galatians 5:14—the golden rule, treat others as you want to be treated. Love others as you want to be loved—or as you love yourself.

Neighbor is an interesting word, isn't it? Our neighbors can be many different people. Sometimes it's the chatty woman bagging our groceries, or the preoccupied man at the stoplight, or even the traumatized woman in Congo. But what about your *neighbors*? You know, the people who actually live next door?

Every day we drive past their homes—every single day. We wave and smile, but never really engage. Surely Jesus doesn't mean these are our neighbors. He was just speaking figuratively, right? We don't think so. We think he was talking about them too.

This week do one thing that shows love to a neighbor.

Jesus asks us to love our neighbor in Matthew 22:39. But we can't love them when we don't know them. This week, prayerfully consider how you could love your actual neighbors and then boldly do one thing that expresses love. Maybe you need to knock on someone's door and introduce yourself for the first time. Or maybe you need to make good on that "we'll have you over for dinner sometime" promise. Or maybe it's a need you can help with. We don't know what you should do, but the Holy Spirit does. Pray and ask him. And then boldly (and probably with a little fear) obey. We have to start the process of loving our neighbor somewhere. Even a little step is a step in the right direction.

OPTIONAL

Memorize Galatians 5:1

It is for freedom that Christ has set us free. Stand firm, then, and do not let yourselves be burdened again by a yoke of slavery.

After completing the exercise, reflect on your experience by answering these questions:

- What did you do? If you had considered doing this in the past, what had kept you from it then?

- How did you feel before, during, and after?

- What did you learn from this experience about God, your neighbor, or yourself?

We've rounded the corner into the "what now" section of Galatians. As you probably recall, the first third of the letter contained Paul's personal defense. The second third provided theological reasons to reject the Judaizers' teaching. And now Paul unpacks how we should live in light of this truth.

He transitions with a powerful and beautiful verse, "It is for freedom that Christ has set us free. Stand firm, then, and do not let yourselves be burdened again by a yoke of slavery" (Galatians 5:1). We've been set free, so live in that freedom. Paul then gives a "stand firm" warning because he knows two things consistently threaten our freedom—sin and legalism.

Sin woos us with half-truths, "Since you're free it doesn't really matter what you do. Jesus paid the price and you are forgiven—so enjoy your life, live a little, indulge the flesh." And then a funny thing happens: that little bitty sin grows bigger and bigger and more consuming until it drives us, owns us, and enslaves us. We know it's true, but we still flirt with sin. We still think we are stronger.

Legalism, on the other hand, fences us in, telling us what to do and when to do it—so we won't stray, of course. Legalism says it has our best interest at heart. But the hurdles get higher and higher. Failure becomes the norm. We wind up defeated and lifeless, crushed and enslaved. We've tried to please God, others, and even ourselves but in the end no one is pleased.

Soul slavery sucks the life out of us. We've all experienced it but Paul says we've been set free. It's time to start living like free people. Embrace your freedom, because when you do, love and gratitude naturally well up and flow out. And as a result, we live loving lives depending on the Holy Spirit. Are you free? Absolutely, 100 percent, yes. Are you living free? Well, that's another question entirely.

SET FREE

1. According to Galatians 3:13, 5:1, and Romans 6:18, what have we been set free from?

[Paul] literally says: "For freedom Christ freed you." Both the noun and the verb are the word "freedom"; freedom is both the means and the end of the Christian life! Everything about the Christian gospel is freedom. Jesus's whole mission was an operation of liberation. And the verb translated "has set us free" is in the aorist tense. In Greek this refers to a single, past action that is now complete.
—Timothy Keller
(*Galatians*, 131)

2. How has Christ set us free (Galatians 3:1, 13)?

Yoke: Literally, the wooden bar that allowed two (or more) draft animals to be coupled so that they might effectively work together. In addition to this literal usage, the Bible frequently uses the term metaphorically to refer to work or bondage.
—*Baker Encyclopedia of the Bible*

3. Paul exhorts the Galatians to stand firm and not be burdened again by a "yoke of slavery" (5:1). Read the definition of *yoke* in the margin. Based on what we've been studying, how were the Judaizers tempting the Galatians to take on a "yoke of slavery"?

4. Before the Galatians became Christ-followers, they were Gentiles (who probably practiced pagan religions). What kinds of practices and philosophies were they enslaved to pre-Christ (Galatians 4:8; 1 Corinthians 12:2)?

5. Have you ever felt yoked to something? Describe what happened and how this felt. If you were able to break this "yoke" how did you do it?

6. Jesus transforms the yoke image from one of slavery to one of freedom. Rewrite Matthew 11:28–30 in your own words. In what ways have you experienced this truth in your faith journey? How have you struggled to experience this truth?

The unsaved person wears a yoke of sin (Lam. 1:14); the religious legalist wears the yoke of bondage (Gal. 5:1); but the Christian who depends on God's grace wears the liberating yoke of Christ.
—Warren Wiersbe (*Bible Exposition Commentary*, 713)

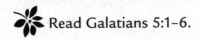

Read Galatians 5:1–6.

DON'T GIVE IN

7. Paul exhorts the Galatians to "stand firm" in their freedom and warns of harsh consequences if they don't. What does he say the consequences are for taking on the Judaizers' yoke of slavery—circumcision (5:2–4)? How do you think these consequences would feel?

8. Have you ever, consciously or subconsciously, taken on legalistic behaviors because you were told, taught, or believed they would earn you benefits from God? What happened? How did it impact your relationship with the Lord?

9. Are there places in your life where you need to "stand firm" so you don't take on a yoke of slavery?

Paul's phrase "fallen away from grace" in 5:4 has fostered much debate. Did Paul believe the Galatians would lose their salvation if they took on the Mosaic law or did he mean something different? We don't think Paul thought they would lose their salvation because he consistently called the Galatians his brothers and sisters, indicating they were grafted into God's family. We think "fallen away from grace" means he worried that by leaving the grace-based faith they started with, they would move to a legalistic works-based system and thereby fall away from grace.

10. Paul has been adamant that the Galatians should not undergo circumcision. Why do you think he said that "neither circumcision nor uncircumcision has any value" (5:6)?

11. Paul finished by saying, "The only thing that counts is faith expressing itself through love." Do you think Paul contradicted himself and advocated for works in this verse? Why or why not?

12. Do you express love as a result of your freedom in Christ? How is this different from times when you act out of obligation or guilt?

Read Galatians 5:7–12.

BE VIGILANT

13. Paul said the Galatians were running a good race until someone cut them off (v. 7). Who cut the Galatians off? How did the Galatians respond?

14. Have you ever been cut off or hindered while you were running? How did you feel? What would happen to your spiritual "race" if you were cut off?

15. Yeast is frequently used in Scripture to represent something evil or false. In verse 9, Paul warns the Galatians that "a little yeast works through the whole batch of dough." During his earthly ministry Jesus warned his followers using similar figurative language in Matthew 16:5–6 and 12. What or who do you think the "yeast" is that both Jesus and Paul are talking about? Why do you think Paul brought up this topic at this time?

16. Roughly how much yeast is used to make a batch of dough rise? What do you think this means about the Judaizers' teaching?

17. Describe a time when a small amount of evil or falsehood grew in your life like yeast. What was the outcome?

Pray and ask the Holy Spirit to reveal any places where you currently have a small amount of something evil or false in your life. Ask the Lord to help you choose him and the truth instead of the "yeast" that you identified.

Speaking out of deep concern for the gospel of the grace of God, Paul uttered a strong expression. He wished that the Judaizers, who were so enthusiastic about circumcision, would go the whole way and castrate themselves, as did the pagan priests of the cult of Cybele in Asia Minor. Perhaps the resulting physical impotence pictured Paul's desire that they also be unable to produce new converts.
—Donald Campbell ("Galatians," 606)

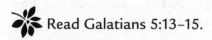

Read Galatians 5:13–15.

FREEDOM TO INDULGE?

18. Compare Galatians 5:1 with 5:13. What are the two pitfalls Paul warned against?

19. In what ways could freedom lead people to sin (5:13)? Have you ever struggled with this? If so, in what ways? What does Romans 6:1–2 say about the idea that freedom could lead to more sin?

20. Instead of indulging in sin, what did Paul call us to do (v. 13)? How do you think serving one another in love counters the temptation to indulge in sin?

21. How did Paul summarize the whole law (v. 14)? Thus far Paul has been proving to the Galatians that they should not live under the law. Why do you think he brought up the law here? Based on what we've learned about the law, do you think he was contradicting himself? Why or why not?

DIGGING DEEPER

Paul describes what serving one another in love looks like in detail in 1 Corinthians 13. Dissect this beautiful text to learn how to live out love in your everyday life. What qualities describe a loving person? Which are most difficult for you? Pick one and ask the Holy Spirit to show you how to live out that quality in your relationships this week.

Walk by the Spirit | LESSON 8

PRACTICE ❀ DAILY EXAMEN

Living in true freedom is enticing. We imagine you want it as much as we do. When we think of freedom, we see ourselves running unhindered with arms stretched wide (and it's also a beautiful day with mountains in the background).

That mental picture isn't too far off. Paul frequently used movement words to describe our faith journey. Often he employed a race metaphor, but in the passage this week he used the consistent, one-foot-in-front-of-the-other word *walk*. Paul said the key to living free is to walk in the Spirit.

How exactly do we walk in the Spirit? We recognize the Spirit's leading and movement in our lives and then follow his lead. Some versions say, "keep in step with the Spirit." This is like walking on the beach behind someone and putting our feet exactly into their footprints.

But we can't put our footprints into the Spirit's until we learn to recognize his footprints. So this week we are going to work on cultivating our attentiveness to the Spirit through an exercise many call a daily examen, which is really just a time to intentionally reflect on where God is at work in our lives.

Often our busyness distracts us from seeing what God is up to. We may briefly notice him in the moment. But then we blaze on, and we've forgotten by bedtime. Taking time to stop and reflect helps us intentionally note God's consistent presence and movement in our lives.

Set aside five to ten minutes each day to reflect on God's movement in your life.

Ask the Holy Spirit to help you recognize his activity in your life, and to help you boldly keep in step with him. You might create a daily chart to record your findings.

OPTIONAL

Memorize
Galatians 5:16, 18

So I say, walk by the Spirit, and you will not gratify the desires of the flesh. . . . But if you are led by the Spirit, you are not under the law.

After completing the exercise, reflect on your experience by answering these questions:

- When did you notice you were most able to live out some aspect of the fruit of the Spirit (love, joy, peace, patience, kindness, goodness, faithfulness, gentleness, and self-control) during your day? Any ideas why?

- When did you notice you were least able to live out some aspect of the fruit of the Spirit during your day? Any ideas why?

- Was there a time during your day when you noticed a strong desire toward sin? What happened?

- Was there a time in your day when you noticed a strong desire toward the Spirit (or righteousness)? What happened?

- Did you sense the Holy Spirit's leading in some way during your day? Did you follow or resist? Why?

The fruit of the Spirit isn't something we can just muscle up the gumption to obtain. Have you ever tried to be more patient? We might experience a few moments of success, but then something happens—like our flight gets delayed (again!) and out plops our impatience. Oops. The true nature of our heart revealed.

But don't be discouraged because it's the Holy Spirit's job to grow this fruit in us. Which means the longer we journey with Jesus, the more we should notice real transformation. And hopefully one day we'll find ourselves in that same situation that elicits impatience, but now our first reaction is actually more patience. The true nature of our heart transformed.

But what if you haven't noticed this growth? Or what if you used to be patient and now suddenly you display that short fuse again? As we'll see, Paul recognized we have a choice. We can choose to live by the Spirit and thereby allow him to grow his fruit in our lives, or we can choose to live by the sinful nature and squelch the Spirit. The Spirit promises to lead us toward freedom, but the sinful nature leads us toward slavery.

This makes choosing the Spirit over sin seem like an easy choice. But we all know it isn't. Sin is alluring and offers us short-term pleasure. Somehow it always convinces us that it won't lead to slavery, that it won't take hold of us, and that we are still in control. It's deceptive and often difficult to resist.

It's not easy to choose a life that keeps in step with the Spirit. It's frequently inconvenient and sacrificial. But if we believe God's Word, a life in step with the Spirit ultimately leads us to a life filled with freedom, characterized by love, joy, peace, patience, kindness, goodness, faithfulness, gentleness, and self-control.

Read Galatians 5:16–25.

COMPETING DESIRES

1. In verses 16–18, what are the two competing forces?

2. Do you think there are any choices that could be considered a middle ground between these two choices? Why or why not?

The Christian's life in all its aspects—intellectual and ethical, devotional and relational, upsurging in worship and outgoing in witness—is supernatural; only the Spirit can initiate and sustain it.
—J. I. Packer (*Keep in Step*, 9)

3. If you choose to walk by the Spirit, what does verse 16 say will happen to the desires of the flesh? Will they go away completely? What do you think this implies about our journey of walking with the Spirit?

DIGGING DEEPER

One of the many ministries of the Spirit involves prayer. Read Romans 8:26–27. What is the Spirit doing for us constantly? How do you feel as you read these verses?

4. Many translations say, "walk by the Spirit" (v. 16). Think about the last time you took an enjoyable walk with someone. What happened? What didn't happen? Do you see any parallels between this and walking by the Spirit?

Literally Paul calls the "desires of the sinful nature" *epithumia*. In older versions, this word was translated "lust," which led the reader to think of sexual desire. In modern translations the word is just translated "desires"; but this may be even more unhelpful.

Literally, *epithumia* means an "over-desire," an "inordinate desire"; an all-controlling drive and longing. This is crucial. The main problem our heart has is not so much desires for bad things, but our over-desires for good things. When a good thing becomes our "god," it creates "over-desires."

—Timothy Keller (*Galatians*, 146)

5. What are some things you desire in your life right now? Are any of them inherently bad? When could these desires cross over to become contrary to what the Spirit desires for you?

6. What do you think Paul means in Galatians 5:18? What does the Spirit lead believers to do (5:16)?

THE SIN NATURE

Paul tells us that when we live by the Spirit we won't give in to sin. Knowing the Galatians probably needed more direction in this area, Paul took the opportunity to list some of the acts of the sin nature in verses 19–21.

7. Many theologians believe Paul was addressing four general categories of sin. Fill in the chart according to the category of sin. (Hint: the order Paul uses is the order used in the chart.)

Category	Sin
Sexual Sins	1. 2. 3.
Religious Sins	1. 2.
Social Sins	1. 2. 3. 4. 5. 6. 7. 8.
Substance Abuse Sins	1. 2.

Sexual immorality (*porneia*) is often translated "fornication." From this word comes the term "pornography." *Porneia* refers to any and all forms of illicit sexual relationships. Impurity (*akatharsia*) is a broad term referring to moral uncleanness in thought, word, and deed (cf. Eph. 5:3–4). Debauchery (*aselgeia*) connotes an open, shameless, brazen display of these evils (cf. 2 Cor. 12:21 where the same words occur; *aselgeia* is included in Rom. 13:13).
—Donald Campbell ("Galatians," 607)

8. Read the different words Paul uses for sexual sins in the sidebar. Why do you think Paul used these three terms when addressing sexual sins?

We are to worship God, love people, and use things, but too often we use people, love self, and worship things, leaving God out of the picture completely.
—Warren Wiersbe (*Bible Exposition Commentary*, 718)

9. The next group of sins is idolatry and witchcraft. Idolatry is allowing anything to take the place of God in your life. How would you define witchcraft (or sorcery, depending on your translation)? Have you ever witnessed or experienced witchcraft or sorcery? What happened?

10. The third group is the social (or relational) sins. Pick one of the eight words from this list in question 7. Look it up in a dictionary, and write the definition below. Where have you observed this sin? What happened and what was the ultimate outcome? If your sharing involves someone else, please be honoring with your words.

11. The final group of sins concerns substance abuse. Read the Timothy Keller quote in the margin. Is all pleasure-seeking wrong? When do you think it crosses the line?

There are two words that refer to substance abuse: drunkenness and orgies. These two words are linked. Orgies are not "sex orgies" but "drinking orgies." One of the works of the flesh is addiction to pleasure-creating substances and behavior.
—Timothy Keller
(*Galatians*, 149)

12. Paul finished the list with the phrase "and the like" to indicate it was not a complete list. Paul wrote this list to address specific sins the Galatians were dealing with in their culture. If Paul was writing to us today, what additional sins do you think he might include in the list?

13. Reread Galatians 5:14. Read through the sin list once more slowly and compare each sin with the law of loving your neighbor. What stands out to you?

14. Which area of sin from question 7 do you tend to struggle with the most? Spend a few moments acknowledging this sin struggle before the Lord. Ask him to help you live by the Spirit in this area so you can experience victory over this sin.

A few passages that speak to our eternal security are John 6:37, John 10:28, Romans 8:38–39, 2 Corinthians 1:22, and Ephesians 2:8.

The apostle then solemnly warned the Galatians . . . that those who live like this, who habitually indulge in these fleshly sins will not inherit the future kingdom of God. This does not say that a Christian loses his salvation if he lapses into a sin of the flesh, but that a person who lives continually on such a level of moral corruption gives evidence of not being a child of God.
—Donald Campbell ("Galatians," 608)

The phrase "will not inherit the kingdom of God" is troubling. Is Paul teaching that we can lose our salvation if we do something on this sin list? We all know (especially from personal experience) that every believer does things on this list, but many Scriptures affirm the security of our salvation (see the sidebar). Considering this, Paul can't mean that we lose our salvation when we sin. So what do we make of this concerning phrase?

Theologians solve this problem in two ways. Some say Paul is referring to someone who regularly and consistently does the things on the sin list, thus proving they were never really believers to begin with (see the Donald Campbell quote in the sidebar for an articulation of this view). This is possible, but problems exist with this solution. For example, how regularly and consistently does one need to sin to prove they were never really a believer?

The second solution, which we prefer, focuses on the word *inherit*. Scripture tells us that we will each receive rewards for the way we've lived our lives. This will happen at the judgment seat of Christ (known as the *bema* seat), and has nothing to do with our receiving or not receiving eternal life. (Remember, that decision is made based on our faith in Christ alone.) This "rewards" judgment is only for believers and happens when Christ returns and establishes the kingdom of God. Therefore, if Paul is talking about inheriting rewards then he isn't referring to our salvation.

15. Read 1 Corinthians 3:11–15. In this passage Paul describes the "day" we receive rewards based on how we have built on the foundation of our faith in Jesus. What two things does he say could happen to our works? What kind of works do you think will survive? What kind of works do you think will be burned up? Either way, what happens to the believer? How does this support a loss of inheritance understanding for Galatians 5:21?

A few additional passages that mention *bema* seat judgment are Romans 14:10–12, 1 Corinthians 4:5, and 2 Corinthians 5:9–10.

FRUIT OF THE SPIRIT

16. Write out the nine aspects of the fruit of the Spirit (5:22–23). Circle the one you tend to exhibit most consistently. Underline the one you most consistently struggle to exhibit.

The contrast between works and fruit is important. A machine in a factory works, and turns out a product, but it could never manufacture fruit. Fruit must grow out of life, and, in the case of the believer, it is the life of the Spirit (Gal. 5:25).
—Warren Wiersbe (*Bible Exposition Commentary*, 719)

DIGGING DEEPER

Paul also writes about the Spirit's ministry in our lives in his letter to the church in Rome. Wring out Romans 8:1–17. What else do you learn about the Spirit's work in the world and in your life?

17. Why do you think you are better at exhibiting some aspects of the fruit of the Spirit than others?

18. Is there an aspect of the fruit of the Spirit that you have noticed growth in over the years? (For example, you are more patient today than you used to be.) What do you think has caused this change? Does this encourage you?

19. Read 1 Corinthians 12:1, 7–11. Why are spiritual gifts given (v. 7; see also 1 Peter 4:10)? How do you think gifts of the Spirit differ from fruit of the Spirit?

20. Write out Galatians 5:24 in your own words. What do you think it means to crucify the flesh? Ask the Lord to help you "crucify" the sin you identified in question 14. List any practical steps you feel led to take.

The works of the flesh know no law, but the fruit of the Spirit need no law.
—Thomas Constable
(*Notes*, 85)

21. Brainstorm some ways you can practically "keep in step" with the Spirit (v. 25). Circle your favorite idea and make a plan to implement it this week. Share this with friends for accountability.

"Crucifying the sinful nature" is really the identification and dismantling of idols. It means to put an end to the ruling and attractive power that idols have in our lives. . . . (It) is about strangling sin at the motivational level, rather than simply setting ourselves against sin at the behavioral level.
—Timothy Keller
(*Galatians*, 155)

Live Out Love | LESSON 9

PRACTICE ✿ BE A BURDEN BEARER

The burden became overwhelming. I (Jodie) had no idea what to do, and worse, I had no idea what would happen. So much was out of my control. I knew I needed a safe place to process so I called a dear friend and found myself at her kitchen table moments later. All my fears tumbled out in a blubbering mess. I'm not sure how many of my words were even coherent. She listened. She didn't try to fix me or placate me. She agreed—the situation was bad. She cried with me.

And then she gave me half of her dinner to take home. "Oh, I made lots extra" she fibbed as she shoved it in my hand. "Please take it. It will give you one less thing to think about tonight."

I went home feeling lighter. Nothing had changed. The circumstances were still the same, and still largely out of my control. Yet, I was reminded I wasn't going to face it alone. It would still be my story—no one could take the circumstances away—but God, my family, and friends were at my side no matter how the story ended.

Some years ago, I (Sue) felt the time bomb ticking inside me. My boss had charged me to lead an important project. Honored, I emailed a key contributor to begin the process, but this gentleman replied back in a rather condescending tone that made it perfectly clear that he would only partner on the project with my boss—I assumed because of my gender. He subtly insinuated that I must be overstepping my bounds to think I wielded that kind of authority in the first place. I was livid—and perplexed as to how to explain the situation to my boss, a dear brother in Christ who trusted me to lead the project well.

As internal pressure grew, I knew I was in danger of doing or saying something unkind, inappropriate, or downright unwise. So I summoned a friend of mine to talk me off the ledge. I unloaded on her long enough to release the steam valve of my pent-up anger. She listened intently, nodding now and then to show me she understood, and then she spoke

OPTIONAL

Memorize Galatians 6:9–10

Let us not become weary in doing good, for at the proper time we will reap a harvest if we do not give up. Therefore, as we have opportunity, let us do good to all people, especially to those who belong to the family of believers.

words of wisdom that restored my perspective and renewed my good sense. We considered wise action plans, and I adopted a good one. Crisis averted (and the offending gentleman and I ended up friends). Both burdens that grieve and burdens that anger need others to help us calm our emotions, regain our perspectives, and act wisely.

We've all had those moments—when the weight of fear, broken dreams, sinful actions, or horrible circumstances comes crashing through our door. Like a bad houseguest, they are not desired or welcomed, but there they are. We have no choice other than to soldier through. But remember, we do not need to soldier alone.

Paul exhorts us in this chapter to bear one another's burdens. And he says that when we do, we fulfill the love of Christ. Bearing burdens is a practical way to love our neighbor.

This week we will do something practical for a friend to help ease their burden.

We all know people bearing incredible burdens. This week ask the Lord to reveal a friend who needs some load-lightening. Once you have a person in mind, ask the Lord what you can do to help. Then make a plan and take steps to accomplish it.

We know some of you feel crushed under your own heavy burdens. If that's you, we challenge you to reach out to someone for help. Often people don't know our burden is crushing us until we speak up. Let a friend know what you need. Give them the opportunity to lighten your load.

My Plan:

who

what

when

After completing the exercise, reflect on your experience by answering these questions:

- Were you able to lighten someone's burden this week? If so, what happened?

- What emotions did you experience as you approached your hurting friend and offered assistance? Why?

- If you needed help bearing your own burden, were you able to ask someone? What happened?

Throughout this study we've seen Paul adamantly advocate for the Galatians to turn away from the claims of the Judaizers and turn back to the gospel. Over and over he challenges us to hold tightly to grace while recognizing our freedom from the law.

But as we've seen, he's not advocating for lawless living. Last week we learned that our freedom in Christ should internally motivate us to live in sync with the Spirit. And life in the Spirit, while often sacrificial and hard, brings fruit, which then brings greater freedom. (It's a beautiful cycle we are wise to embrace.)

Now Paul moves us into a section that's incredibly practical. He speaks to the Galatians about how life lived in the Spirit should look. He addresses division, confrontation, a proper view of self, helping, and comparison. He chose these specific topics because the original audience was dealing with them. Whew! That means they don't apply to us then? I mean we don't know any Christians who deal with division, or sin, or comparison . . .

Kidding. Obviously, we still deal with every single topic Paul presents in the conclusion of his letter. While they were specific to the Galatians, they are timely for us too. So get ready to get practical. This week will be chock-full of ways to live in the Spirit.

Read Galatians 5:26–6:5.

WARNING, WARNING!

In Galatians 5, Paul outlined that a life in step with the Spirit yields fruit and freedom. Now we find a shift to the practicalities of what this looks like, specifically in our relationships.

1. What are the three things that Paul warns us to avoid (5:26)? Look up the word *conceited* and write a short definition. Have you ever known someone you would characterize as conceited? How does this person act? (Please be discreet if you share in your group.)

2. The original text implies two ways we become conceited: by provoking or envying. Read the Timothy Keller quote in the margin for definitions. How is provocation an outworking of conceit? How is envy an outworking of conceit? Which do you struggle with more?

"Provoke" . . . is competitive, meaning to challenge someone to a contest. "Envy" means to want something that rightfully belongs to someone else, or to want that person to not have that thing.
—Timothy Keller (*Galatians*, 160)

3. We may not be considered conceited, but we all struggle to some extent with self-preoccupation. What do you think causes this preoccupation? Where do you struggle?

According to Paul this preoccupation expresses itself as either a superior or inferior attitude. We express superior conceit (provocation) when we believe we are winning and fear losing this position. We experience inferior conceit (envy) when we believe we are losing and think no one notices.

4. Why do you think Paul places the stern warning of Galatians 5:26 right after his exhortation to walk in the Spirit and not the flesh?

THE ART OF GENTLE RESTORATION

5. What do you think it means to restore a person gently (6:1)? How does this support Galatians 5:13–14?

If your brother or sister sins, go and point out their fault, just between the two of you. If they listen to you, you have won them over. But if they will not listen, take one or two others along, so that "every matter may be established by the testimony of two or three witnesses." If they still refuse to listen, tell it to the church; and if they refuse to listen even to the church, treat them as you would a pagan or a tax collector.
—Jesus (Matthew 18:15–17)

6. The person who is to "restore gently" must "live by the Spirit" (6:1; also see 5:22–23). Do you think this is important? Why or why not?

Matthew 18:15–17 contains Scripture's most direct teaching about the difficult task of resolving conflict. Jesus commands Christians to face conflict head-on, laying out steps designed to lead to reconciliation, peace, and harmony.
—Sue Edwards & Kelley Mathews, *Leading Women Who Wound*, 116

7. According to Matthew 7:3–5, what should we do before we aim to restore someone caught in sin?

DIGGING DEEPER

Dissect the sidebar containing Jesus's instructions when we enter into a conflict with a brother or sister in Christ. What three steps are embedded in these verses? Write out what these steps might actually look like in a conflict you've experienced. How could following Jesus's mandate help you the next time you experience conflict?

8. Why do you think Paul added the warning, "But watch yourselves, or you also may be tempted"? In what ways could you be tempted when you set out to restore your brother or sister in Christ?

Nothing makes us feel so righteous as exposing another person's glaring evil, especially if it is an evil we are never tempted to do.
—Bowen Matthews ("Conviction and Compassion")

9. Does Matthew 7:3–5 mean you should attempt to restore anyone caught in sin (both believers and unbelievers)? Why or why not?

Does this passage mean you should attempt to restore your brothers and sisters every time you see them sin? Why or why not?

How will you decide moving forward if you should attempt to restore someone? When you do attempt to restore someone, what should always be your aim?

The expression "law of Christ" is surprising in its formulation since Paul has spent a great deal of time dismissing the law as the Christian's guide. Nonetheless, his willingness to say Christians are under the "law of Christ" and not the "law of Moses" is entirely reasonable. . . . The Christian's law is following Jesus, that is, living in submission to the Spirit.
—Scot McKnight (*NIV Application Commentary*, 285)

BURDEN BEARING

10. What is the law of Christ (Galatians 6:2; 5:14; Matthew 22:37–39)? In what ways do you think bearing each other's burdens fulfills the law of Christ?

11. Fill in the blanks below based on Galatians 6:2–5.

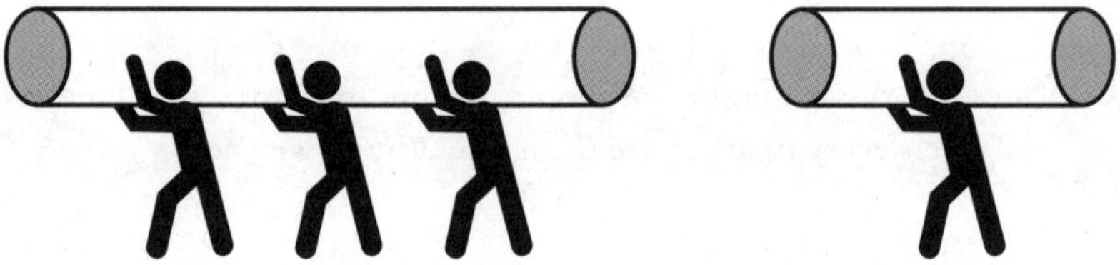

Carry each others' ____________

Each one should carry their own ___________

A **burden** (v. 2) is a "heavy, crushing load (*baré*)—more than a man could carry without help" and a **load** (v. 5) is the "Greek word (*phortion*) . . . used to designate the pack usually carried by a marching soldier."
—Donald Campbell ("Galatians," 610)

12. Read the definitions of the original words for *burden* and *load* in the sidebar. When do you think a load becomes a burden? Write some of the burdens you have had to carry in the past or are currently carrying on the first illustration in question 11. Did you have help shouldering this burden? If so, what difference did it make? What was the helper able to do and unable to do?

13. What are some burdens you are currently carrying (or will always carry) that you think constitute your "own load"? Write these on the second illustration in question 11. Is there anything in your life that seems to switch back and forth between "load" and "burden"? If so, what? What seems to make the difference?

14. What do you think Galatians 6:6 means? What are some practical ways to do this?

Read Galatians 6:7–10.

REAPING AND SOWING

15. Why do you think Paul begins this section of his letter with the warning that God cannot be mocked? How does a person who sows to please their sin nature (or flesh) mock God (v. 7)?

In farming or gardening, this is an absolute principle, and Paul appears to want us to see at least two aspects to it. First, *whatever* you sow, you will reap. If you sow tomato seeds, you will not get corn, no matter how much you want corn to grow! Second, whatever you sow, you *will* reap. Though the seed may lie in the ground to no apparent effect for a long time, it will come up. It is not the reaping that determines the harvest, but the sowing.
—Timothy Keller
(*Galatians*, 175

16. Have you ever reaped a harvest of "destruction" (v. 8) because you sowed to please your sin nature? What happened? At the time, did you deceive yourself into believing you could reap a different harvest than the one you received?

DIGGING DEEPER

What do you learn in 1 Corinthians 2:6–16 about ways the Holy Spirit reveals God's will in our lives as we attempt to keep in step with him? How might this knowledge help you sow to please the Spirit in your life this week?

17. Based on what we've been learning in this study, what do you think it means to "sow to please the Spirit" (v. 8)?

If we want His direction for our decisions, the great cravings of our souls must not only be the big moments of assignment. They must also be the seemingly small instructions in the most ordinary of moments when God points His Spirit finger saying, Go there.
—Lysa TerKeurst
(*The Best Yes*, 16)

18. Read Thomas Constable's explanation of the two meanings of eternal life in the sidebar. Based on these definitions and your own understanding of eternal life, how do you think sowing in the Spirit reaps eternal life?

The term "eternal life" has two different, though related, meanings in the New Testament. Essentially it is the life of God that He shares with believers. On the one hand, the New Testament writers spoke of it as a gift that one receives by faith. . . . However, it also refers to the quality of the believer's life, that depends on the extent to which he or she walks with God in fellowship.
—Thomas Constable (*Notes*, 93)

19. Are we promised to reap a harvest if we do good (v. 9)? What kind of harvest will we reap? When might we reap it? How does this encourage or discourage you?

Read Galatians 6:11–18.

CLOSING REMARKS

Paul presumably pulls the quill from his scribe's hand to finish off his letter. Many scholars suppose that his "large letters" indicate emphasis. This is Paul's final plea to the church of Galatia and to us.

20. According to Paul, why are the Judaizers trying to compel the Galatians to be circumcised (6:12–13)? In contrast, why does Paul "boast" (v. 14)?

21. What does Paul call his teaching in the letter to the Galatians (v. 16)? And if we follow it, what will result? How would you sum up this "rule" or "principle"?

22. Paul closes by saying he bears the "marks" of Jesus. What mark did the Judaizers say they bore (6:12)? In what way was Paul marked or scarred for Jesus (see 2 Corinthians 11:23–27 and Acts 14:19, which happened in the region of Galatia)? What do you think Paul is saying? Have you been marked or scarred for Jesus (physically or emotionally)? If so, how?

23. Paul states his final sign-off in verse 18. In what ways does this verse summarize some of the major themes of the book?

But when grace and truth were realized through Jesus Christ, a long-awaited revolution of the heart began to set religious captives free. Fearful bondage motivated by guilt was replaced by a fresh motivation to follow Him in truth and simply out of deep devotion and delight. Rather than focusing on the accomplishments of the flesh, He spoke of the heart. Instead of demanding that the sinner fulfill a long list of requirements, He emphasized faith, if only the size of a mustard seed. The change spelled freedom, as the Lord Himself taught, ". . . you shall know the truth, and the truth shall make you free" (John 8:32).
—Charles Swindoll
(*Grace Awakening*, 7–8)

24. What are some words or phrases you would use to summarize the book of Galatians?

We hope you have started to grasp the truths of Galatians. It's all about the freedom you have in Christ. You have been released and now you can choose freedom or you can go back into slavery. We so desperately want you to choose freedom. We hope you will make this choice over and over again. Stay vigilant. Freedom isn't easy, but it's always worth it. Go forth, our free friends. You are released.

Works Cited

Baker Encyclopedia of the Bible. Edited by Walter A. Elwell. 4 volumes. Grand Rapids: Baker, 1997.

Braiker, Harriet. *The Disease to Please: Curing the People-Pleasing Syndrome.* New York: McGraw-Hill, 2001.

Campbell, Donald K. "Galatians." In *The Bible Knowledge Commentary: New Testament.* Edited by John F. Walvoord and Roy B. Zuck. Colorado Springs: David C. Cook, 1983.

Constable, Thomas L. *Notes on Galatians.* 2017 edition. www.soniclight.com/constable/notes/pdf/galatians.pdf. Used by permission.

Edwards, Sue, and Kelley Mathews. *Leading Women Who Wound: Strategies for an Effective Ministry.* Chicago: Moody Publishers, 2009.

George, Bob. *Classic Christianity: Life's Too Short to Miss the Real Thing.* Eugene, OR: Harvest House, 1989.

Hirshkowitz, Max, Kaitlyn Whiton, Steven M. Albert et al. "National Sleep Foundation's Sleep Time Duration Recommendations: Methodology and Results Summary." *Sleep Health* 1, no. 1 (March 2015): 40–43. https://doi.org/10.1016/j.sleh.2014.12.010.

Johnson, S. Lewis. "The Paralysis of Legalism." *Bibliotheca Sacra* 120, no. 47 (April–June 1963): 109.

Keller, Timothy. *Galatians for You.* Purcellville, VA: The Good Book Company, 2013.

Lewis, C. S. *The Problem of Pain.* New York: MacMillan, 1962.

Longenecker, Richard N. *Galatians.* Word Biblical Commentary Series. Dallas: Word Books, 1990.

Lucado, Max. *In the Grip of Grace: You Can't Fall Beyond His Love.* Dallas: Word Publishing, 1996.

MacArthur, John. *Galatians: The Wondrous Grace of God.* Nashville: Thomas Nelson, 2007.

Matthews, S. Bowen. "Conviction and Compassion." In *The Art and Craft of Biblical Preaching: A Comprehensive Resource for Today's Communicators.* Edited by Haddon Robinson and Craig Brian Larson. Grand Rapids: Zondervan, 2005.

McKnight, Scot. *The NIV Application Commentary: Galatians.* Grand Rapids: Zondervan, 1995.

Millikin, Jimmy A. "Grace." In *Holman Illustrated Bible Dictionary.* Edited by Charles W. Draper, Chad Brand, and Archie England. Nashville: Holman Bible Publishers, 2003.

Packer, J. I. *Keep in Step with the Spirit.* Old Tappan, NJ: Fleming H. Revell, 1984.

Patterson, Ben. *Waiting: Finding Hope When God Seems Silent.* Downers Grove, IL: InterVarsity Press, 1989.

Schreiner, Thomas R. *Galatians.* Exegetical Commentary on the New Testament. Grand Rapids: Zondervan, 2010.

Swindoll, Charles R. *The Grace Awakening.* Dallas: Word Publishing, 1990.

TerKeurst, Lysa. *The Best Yes: Making Wise Decisions in the Midst of Endless Demands.* Nashville: Thomas Nelson, 2014.

Wiersbe, Warren W. *The Bible Exposition Commentary: New Testament.* Volume 1. Colorado Springs: Cook Communications, 2001.

Winebrenner, Jan. *Intimate Faith: A Woman's Guide to the Spiritual Disciplines.* New York: Warner Books, 2003.

Wright, N. T. *Galatians: 10 Studies for Individuals and Groups.* Downers Grove, IL: InterVarsity Press, 2010.

Yancey, Philip. *What's So Amazing About Grace?* Grand Rapids: Zondervan, 1997.

About the Authors

Sue Edwards is associate professor of educational ministries and leadership (her specialization is women's studies) at Dallas Theological Seminary, where she has the opportunity to equip men and women for future ministry. She brings over forty years of experience into the classroom as a Bible teacher, curriculum writer, and overseer of several megachurch women's ministries. As minister to women at Irving Bible Church and director of women's ministry at Prestonwood Baptist Church in Dallas, she has worked with women from all walks of life, ages, and stages. Her passion is to see modern and postmodern women connect, learn from one another, and bond around God's Word. Her Bible studies have ushered thousands of women all over the country and overseas into deeper Scripture study and community experiences.

With Kelley Mathews, Sue has coauthored *New Doors in Ministry to Women: A Fresh Model for Transforming Your Church, Campus, or Mission Field*; *Women's Retreats: A Creative Planning Guide*; and *Leading Women Who Wound: Strategies for an Effective Ministry*. Sue and Kelley joined with Henry Rogers to coauthor *Mixed Ministry: Working Together as Brothers and Sisters in an Oversexed Society*. Her newest book, coauthored with Barbara Neumann, *Organic Mentoring: A Mentor's Guide to Relationships with Next Generation Women*, explores the new values, preferences, and problems of the next generation and shows mentors how to avoid potential land mines and how to mentor successfully.

Sue has a doctor of ministry degree from Gordon-Conwell Theological Seminary in Boston and a master's in Bible from Dallas Theological Seminary. With Dr. Joye Baker, she oversees the Dallas Theological Seminary doctor of ministry degree in Christian education with a women-in-ministry emphasis.

Sue has been married to David over forty-five years. They have two married daughters, Heather and Rachel, and five grandchildren. David is a retired CAD applications engineer, a lay prison chaplain and founder of their church's prison ministry, and now a DTS student. Sue loves fine chocolates and exotic coffees, romping with her grandchildren, aquasize, and taking walks with David and her two West Highland terriers, Wallace and Emma Jane.

Jodie Niznik is pastor of leadership development and women's teaching at Irving Bible Church in Irving, Texas. She has served in various roles on the pastoral team at her church over the last nine years, including pastor to women. Her calling and passion is to equip people to take the next step in their journey with Jesus. She loves to write about and teach scriptural truths in practical and easy-to-understand ways.

Jodie started her educational journey pursuing a degree in physics, but quickly realized she would make a horrible physicist when the basic laws of motion and gravity began to confound her. She moved from formulas to words and graduated with a broadcast journalism degree. Later she earned a master of Christian education degree with an emphasis in women's ministry from Dallas Theological Seminary. She is the author of three additional Bible studies: *Choosing a Life that Matters: A Study of Moses*; *Follow: Peter's Journey with Jesus*; and *Pursuit: The Story of God's Love for His People.*

Jodie is married to Tim, who with a PhD in mathematics obviously understands numbers better than she does. They have two young-adult daughters, Taylor and Billie, who recently left the nest to attend universities in Oklahoma and Arkansas. Jodie and Tim miss their daughters but love their quiet Saturdays. Jodie believes gummy bears and coffee are sweet gifts from the Lord that provide fuel as she writes Bible studies and prepares biblical teachings.